★ BEN MYERS' ★

BEST
American
BEERS

YBOR CITY
YCBC
BREWING COMPANY

CLB

★ BEN MYERS' ★

BEST
American
BEERS

**AN ENTHUSIAST'S GUIDE TO THE MOST
DISTINCTIVE CRAFT BREWS OF THE US AND CANADA**

Edited and compiled by Benjamin Myers

Contributors: Lew Bryson, Phil and Sara Doersam, Tom Dalldorf and Stephen Beaumont

DEDICATION

*To my parents, Hyman and Sandra Myers, for their unflagging
enthusiasm, encouragement, and support (despite my rather odd career choices).*

CREDITS

EDITOR Philip de Ste. Croix   DESIGN Louise Clements
DESIGN MANAGER Justina Leitão   DIRECTOR OF EDITORIAL Will Steeds   PRODUCTION Neil Randles Karen Staff
COLOR REPRODUCTION Pica Colour Separations, Singapore   PRINTED AND BOUND IN SINGAPORE by Star Standard Industries

5128 Ben Myers' Best American Beers
Produced by CLB International

This edition published in 1999 by CLB, an imprint of
Quadrillion Publishing Limited, Godalming Business Centre,
Woolsack Way, Godalming, Surrey GU7 1XW, UK

Distributed in the USA by Quadrillion Publishing Inc.
230 Fifth Avenue, New York, NY 10001
© Copyright 1999 Quadrillion Publishing Limited
All rights reserved.
No part of this publication may be reproduced, stored in a
retrieval system or transmitted by any means, electronic, mechanical,
photocopying or otherwise, without the prior permission of
the copyright owner.
ISBN 1-84100-137-6

PICTURE CREDITS

Unless otherwise credited below, all the pictures
in this book were supplied by the featured breweries.

The publisher would like to acknowledge, with warm thanks,
the co-operation of everyone who has supplied the
illustrations reproduced. Thanks also to the following
individuals who supplied photographs from their collections:
pp.23, 27, 29: Larry C. Volk;
p.35: Peter Vanderwarker; p.105: William J. Covaleski;
p.107: William Rutledge; p.156: Jerry Capps;
pp. 167, 315: Nick Sholley;
pp.193, 197, 211: Foto Imagery/Tim Murphy;
p.301: Alan Hicks;
p.375: Stephen Beaumont.

Benjamin Myers, co-author of *The Encyclopedia Of World Beers* (Chartwell Books, 1997), has written broadly on beer for publications such as *The Washington Post*, *The Philadelphia Inquirer*, *Gourmet* magazine, and Britain's *Sunday Telegraph*. He also has contributed to many consumer beer journals such as *All About Beer*, *The Celebrator Beer News*, *What's Brewing* (UK), *BarleyCorn*, and *Ale Street News*. He writes a column ("Beersay") for the *Malt Advocate*.

Mr. Myers received America's prestigious James Beard Journalism Award for "Newspaper Writing on Spirits, Wine & Beer" in 1996, and was nominated for a 1995 James Beard Journalism Award. He also was named "Beer Writer Of The Year" in 1996 by the North American Guild of Beer Writers. After time in Philadelphia, San Francisco, London, and Oxford, Benjamin Myers now lives in Seattle, Washington. In addition to his writing, he has handled marketing communications for Pyramid Breweries, as well as the premium wine company behind Chateau Ste. Michelle, Columbia Crest, and Bert Grant's Ales. He is a graduate of Stanford University.

Contents

Introduction......10

Introduction

From Texas to Toronto, a guide to the best of American and Canadian brewing.

Britain can claim the honors, thanks to its CAMRA (Campaign for Real Ale) consumer movement, for launching the modern ale renaissance during the 1970s. But credit for the overall specialty beer revolution rests squarely with North America. Sure, the continent's national brewers continue to roll out their infamously bland "Pilsner" brands. But a growing group of small breweries have together done more to revitalize classic beer styles and innovate new ones than all the world's other brewers put together. From Boston to British Columbia, from Toronto to Texas, creative North American brewers bear the standard of the world's beer revolution.

Today, there are more small breweries in America — close to 1,300, up from only 60 in 1975 — than anywhere else around the globe. American drinkers now hoist hoppy pale ales with one hand, and rich, dark lagers with the other.

Canadian beer-lovers enjoy everything from malty Irish-style ales to Belgian-style cherry brews. Bavarian hefeweizens come from Colorado, while oatmeal stouts are quaffed in Quebec. And that's not even scratching the surface of North America's burgeoning beer variety.

Coming after decades of pale, fizzy neglect, this beer revolution recalls the early centuries of North American brewing – a time when waves of European settlers first brought the ales, and later the lagers, of their homelands to the shores of their New World. Indigenous Americans had their own robust "brews," of course: echoes of these survive in the *chicha* corn-brews still enjoyed by natives in Mexico and South America. But beer as we know it today arrived with the Europeans.

All of the early North American breweries made ales in the styles of the day:

porters, stouts, even the then–new "pale" varieties. When waves of German and Eastern European immigrants began arriving in the mid–1800s, the tide turned towards the "lager" beers that were captivating beer halls from Berlin to Budapest. Soon, thousands of local breweries were offering beers in either or both varieties. The result was a vibrant, thriving North American brewing scene.

And then Prohibition arrived.

The Temperance movement of the early 20th century proved particularly sobering for North America's brewers. In both the United States and Canada (with the notable exception of Quebec), laws banned the production and sale of alcoholic beverages. Some brewers survived on legal low–alcohol brews ("near beer"), while others turned to related industries. Colorado's Coors made malted milk, and Anheuser-Busch produced ice cream at several of its refrigerated plants. But the majority of North American breweries closed their doors forever.

It has been said of Prohibition brews that whoever coined the term "near beer" was a poor judge of distance.

When Prohibition ended in 1933, the North American beer industry was but a shadow of its former frothy glory. Aggressive breweries exploited the situation, expanding both their markets and marketing strategies. In Canada, for example, the post-Prohibition combine called Canadian Breweries (later Carling O'Keefe) absorbed more than 20 independent breweries across Ontario and Quebec in an effort to build its market share. America's bigger breweries focused on producing "national brands" that were meant to appeal to the broadest possible tastes, across the broadest possible market areas.

By the 1970s, the American brewing industry was dominated by an elite circle of "megabrewers" (Pabst, Anheuser-Busch, Coors, Miller, Stroh, Heileman, Schlitz, to name a few). Across the border, Carling, Molson, and Labatt controlled Canadian brewing. Molson at least had the historical distinction of being the continent's oldest operating brewery (founded in 1786). But in terms

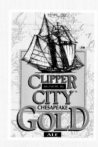

LEFT: *Copper vessels are a time-honored sign of quality and craftsmanship.*

15

1998 saw America's total number of breweries finally surpass longtime leader Germany's – to the dismay of Teutonic tipplers

of distinctiveness, of character, things looked bleak for North American beer. And then the beery worm began to turn.

The late 1970s saw America slowly embrace a new wave of small brewers (companies so tiny, in fact, that they initially were called "boutique" or "micro–" breweries). New Albion, the first recognized North American microbrewery, rolled out its premier barrel from California's "New World" wine country in 1977. At the same time, idiosyncratic brews from surviving regional producers – San Francisco's Anchor Brewing, for example, and Pennsylvania's Yuengling Brewery (the oldest operating brewery in America) – started to recapture the public's attention.

Like many trailblazers, New Albion unfortunately proved ahead of its time. But its pioneering efforts to offer flavorful ales inspired a host of followers across America and Canada. Many of these "original" micros have prospered: early

names like Sierra Nevada and Big Rock now loom large in their once-tiny industry. Overall, the growth of small brewers has been staggering. Successful small brewers have abandoned their "micro" moniker for the more encompassing term "craft-brewer."

ABOVE: *A recipe for good times: sunshine, suds, and smiling friends (here at California's Mendocino Brewing).*

The popularity of micros has not been lost on the megabrewers, despite continuing emphasis on their bland flagship brands and further industry consolidation (Anheuser-Busch, Miller, Coors, and Stroh now dominate America, while Molson and Labatt compose Canada's "Big Two"). Eager to enter the craft-beer arena, both Anheuser-Busch and Miller have bought into a few successful small brewers. And both, along with Coors, Stroh, and Molson, also have introduced "craft beers" of their own: Michelob Hefeweizen, Blue

Moon Belgian White, Henry Weinhard's Blackberry Wheat, and more! While micro-enthusiasts frequently bemoan such actions, the overall result has been a greater choice of more distinctive beers for the average consumer.

At the same time, however, craft-beer supply finally has grown to match (or even outstrip) demand. After years of double-digit growth, small brewers saw their market share stall in 1998 at about three percent of total American beer sales. Perhaps confused by the proliferation of labels and styles, consumers appear to be turning back to "safe" brands they know – both mainstream and, to a much higher degree, imports. Has the microbrew bubble burst? Probably not. Once acquired, a taste for flavorful beer does not disappear overnight. But market reality appears to be catching up with the maturing craft-beer industry. There is no doubt that specialty beers are here to stay. The real question is which specialty brewers are. *This book is a guide to the best bets.*

Given the dynamic nature of the American and Canadian beer scene — start-ups, failures, mergers, and more — an exhaustive study of breweries and brewpubs probably is beyond the scope of any book. Even a limited review would stretch the capabilities of a single author, in light of the changes that seem to occur weekly in this creative industry. In an attempt to provide the most thorough, most up-to-date coverage, this book presents recommendations from a network of highly-qualified writers, each a specialist in their specific areas: Lew Bryson (author of *Pennsylvania Breweries*) on the Northeast and mid-Atlantic states; Phil and Sara Doersam (founders of *Southern Draft Brew News*) on the Southeast, Midwest, and Southwest; Tom Dalldorf (publisher of *The Celebrator Beer News*) on California; and Stephen Beaumont (author of the *Great Canadian Beer Guide*, *A Taste For Beer*, and other books) on his home country of Canada. Entries are organized by region as a result.

A sage once compared specialty beers to sport utility vehicles – the only growing segment of an otherwise-static industry

RIGHT: *Brewers have traditionally built equipment from copper because of the metal's high heat conductivity.*

20

The breweries profiled represent the industry's most noteworthy, chosen based on distinctiveness – in terms of their beers, their reputations, or, usually, both. The majority are full-production facilities (as opposed to stand-alone brewpubs) with beers for sale in bottles and kegs. To help direct readers, each profile offers a list of up to three "recommended" brews that are particularly enjoyable. At the end of each region's entries, an "Also Worth Trying" section explores other worthwhile breweries and beers that, either for space or other considerations, did not receive greater treatment.

Overall, the book provides a colorful snapshot of the American and Canadian craft-beer industry. We hope that it will serve as an exciting introduction for new beer lovers and a reliable reference for experienced fans.

Cheers!

Benjamin Myers, Seattle, Washington

NORTHEAST

long with the mid-Atlantic states, the Northeast possesses strong Colonial-based ale traditions — not surprising, perhaps, in a region known as New England. The area's beer history and local "Yankee pride" have helped it become the country's most fertile microbrewing region outside of the Pacific Northwest. Today, the Northeast hosts a celebrated number of small craft-brewers and the headquarters of America's largest (the Boston Beer Company).

Brewpubs and draft-only micros abound in New England. Relative newcomers exist side-by-side with established pioneers: Massachusetts' Berkshire Brewing and Harpoon Brewery, for example, and Maine's Allagash and D.L. Geary Brewing. Echoing the national pattern, veterans continue to expand production while newcomers (especially brewpubs) still seem to open for business every year.

Overall, Northeast ales retain a more "English" accent than their Northwest counter-parts. This orientation stems, in part, from the fact that many New England brewers use equipment and an (in)famous British Ringwood yeast provided by Peter Austin & Partners, a brewery-installation company originally based in Hampshire, England. But ales are not alone in the Northeast: several brewers also offer classic lager styles or hybrids such as German-inspired altbiers.

Between bowls of clam "chowdah" and weekends at "the shore," thirsty New Englanders keep tabs on the region's beer scene by reading *Yankee Brew News* (P.O. Box 973, Brattleboro, VT 05302) and *Ale Street News* (see Mid-Atlantic).

EST. 1995
100 Industrial Way,
Portland,
Maine 04103
Tel: (207) 878 5385

RECOMMENDED
White
(5.5%),
cloudy, crisp,
citrus-coriander
classic

ALLAGASH BREWING COMPANY

Like Robert Fulghrum's time in kindergarten, founder Rob Todd learned everything he needed to know at Otter Creek. A year's work there, started as a hold-over job while he pondered graduate geology programs, taught him to concentrate on process and patience. One year to

the day after leaving Otter Creek – after a year of single-handedly building a brewery, 80-hour weeks, and two slipped discs – Rob sat down and drank the first pint of Allagash White served on tap at a Portland bar. "I thought, OK, now I have to get back to work," Rob laughs.

Allagash, named for a wild river in northern Maine, produces only three beers: White, Double, and Grand Cru. The White is a classic witbier style, spiked with coriander and bitter orange peel and deceptively quaffable. The Double is perhaps a little more funky on draft than the best Belgian versions; it will age well in the bottle to a richly complex mix of chocolate, malt, and raisins, teasingly on the edge of cloying at first, but drying out nicely with time. The winter seasonal Grand Cru is almost a blend of the other two, with less malt character than the Double and a touch more sweetness than the White. Total production of 1,250 barrels (1,470hl) in 1997 means Allagash is no raging river of beer. But you can bet Rob's working on it.

"White" beer, like other Belgian styles, preserves an old tradition of brewing beer with spices instead of hops alone.

25

ATLANTIC COAST BREWING

★

EST. 1994
50 Terminal Street,
Boston,
Massachusetts 02129
Tel: (617) 242 6464

RECOMMENDED
Tremont Ale
(4.8%), best when
cask-conditioned
Tremont India
Pale Ale
(6.4%), complex,
fruity, with citrus
hop notes
Old Scratch
Barley Wine
(9%), notes of
chocolate, cherry,
and roasted malt

Atlantic Coast Brewing operates under its Tremont Brewery banner, which reflects the three-hill area of Boston where it is located. It is dedicated to producing English-style ales, including the use of imported barley malt, East Kent Golding and Fuggles hops, and a British ale yeast (Ringwood, but with a mellow character for the strain) in open fermenters. Tremont's stainless steel brewing vessels, imported from England, produced around 4,000 barrels (4,700hl) in 1998. Distribution is limited to eastern Massachusetts,

RIGHT: *Once draft-only, as rows of kegs attest, several of Tremont Brewery's beers now are bottled as well.*

but the 1998 hiring of New England beer maven Peter Terhune as marketing director should help raise Tremont's profile outside the area.

The flagship Tremont Ale, which displays a pleasant "Burtonized" character, reaches its peak of flavor when cask-conditioned – the brewery imported actual British casks for this purpose. A handful of Boston-area accounts, including a characterful city pub called Cornwall's, carry the beer in this form (look for tell-tale pumps mounted on the bar). Tremont occasionally cask-conditions small amounts of its other beers, including the holiday season's excellent Old Scratch. In keeping with English barley wine tradition, sugar is added to the brew kettle to enhance this brew's original gravity (1.097 in 1997, 1.098 in 1998, etc.). Tremont

IPA is brewed to the style's appropriate strength and aggressively hopped with Fuggles, Styrian Goldings, and Cascades. The result is a full-bodied, complex ale with a citrusy, aromatic hop character. Other seasonal releases include a dry, roasty Porter (early spring), nutty ESB (fall), and strong Winter Ale (7.1%) with an enjoyable resemblance to England's Old Peculier.

RIGHT: *Tremont's Jeff Biegert checks the specific gravity of a fermenting batch.*

EST. 1994
12 Railroad Street,
South Deerfield,
Massachusetts,
Tel: (413) 665 6600

RECOMMENDED
Steel Rail Extra
Pale Ale
(5.25%), light,
crisp, satisfying
Berkshire Pale Ale
(6.3%), glowing
synergy of hops
and esters

BERKSHIRE BREWING COMPANY

The philosophy of Berkshire Brewing president Chris Lalli – despite his former occupation as a salesman – seems perfectly matched to the honest, hard-working traditions of the brewery's home in Massachusetts' Pioneer Valley. "Brew clean, quality beer. And ours is the cleanest around," he says plainly. "Be good to your local customers. Don't give anything away."

With four years of steady growth leading to a major brewhouse expansion in 1998, he clearly has a recipe (or recipes) for success. That may explain why he is shown smiling on the brewery's labels.

Berkshire started brewing with their briskly-refreshing Steel Rail Extra Pale Ale, then added the bigger Berkshire Pale Ale. Other beers have joined the twin flagships: Lost

Sailor IPA, hearty Drayman's Porter, a strong (6.5%), American-styled Independence Wheat, and Coffeehouse Porter brewed with organic coffee beans. The line is anchored by three heavy-hitting beers: an Imperial Stout, a creative Raspberry Barleywine, and the winter seasonal Holidale (an 8.5% malt-accented barleywine).

Visitors to this beautiful area of woods and ridges will be able to sample Berkshire's beers in a new on-site pub (opening in 1999). Production currently runs fewer than 5,000 barrels (5,870hl) per year, with distribution limited to the home state and Connecticut.

Mt. Greylock, the highest point in the Berkshire hills of western Massachusetts, reaches 3,491 feet at its peak.

EST. 1985
The Brewery,
30 Germania Street,
Boston,
Massachusetts 02130
Tel: (617) 522 3400

RECOMMENDED
Samuel Adams
Cream Stout
(5%), mellow "cap-
puccino" of stout
Samuel Adams
Scotch Ale
(6%), lots of rich malt
and smoky notes
Samuel Adams
Double Bock
(8.4%), richly malty
with chocolate hints

BOSTON BEER COMPANY

Harvard-educated marketer Jim Koch (pronounced "Cook") has turned Boston Beer's family of Samuel Adams ales and lagers into America's best-known microbrews. At the same time, Koch's "major league" market-ing techniques (radio, billboards, television) and unrepentant con-tract-brewing— at mega-plants such as Pittsburgh Brewing, Genesee Brewing, Stroh Brewing, and Blitz-Weinhard Brewing— have vilified the company in the eyes of smaller craft-brewers.

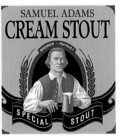

Distribution is inter-national (including Australia and Britain), with annual production over 1,000,000 barrels

RIGHT: *Brewer Jim Pericles demonstrates Boston's "hands-on" style.*

(1,173,000hl). Boston Beer went public in 1995 and trades on the New York Stock Exchange.

The company's original Samuel Adams Boston Lager, named after the Colonial American brewer and patriot, remains its flagship: a well-made amber brew seasoned with German Hallertau and Tettnanger hops (particularly notable when fresh). Other year-round Sam Adams beers include a smooth Cream Stout, robust Scotch Ale (brewed with a notable percentage of peat-smoked malt), and gentle Golden Pilsner. Seasonals encompass spring's lush Double Bock (among the absolute best of its kind in America), a traditional Oktoberfest, and annually-changing Winter Lager. A faintly-spiced Summer Ale was introduced in 1996, a witbier-inspired White Ale in 1998. The company also offers a supremely potent (17.5%), port-like, top-fermented "Triple Bock."

Boston Beer runs its own small brewery – the former Haeffenreffer plant – in Boston, as well as the former Hudepohl-Schoenling Brewery in Cincinnati, Ohio. It has a stake in Philadelphia's Samuel Adams BrewHouse brewpub, and also backs a west coast contract-brewing operation called Oregon Ale & Beer Co. and the HardCore line of ciders.

RIGHT: *Boston Beer's showplace Beantown brewery follows a classic design.*

EST. 1986
P.O. Box 754,
Windsor Industrial
Park, Windsor,
Vermont 05089
Tel: (800) 540 2248

RECOMMENDED
Porter
(5.3%), extremely soft,
quaffable,
chocolatey, and fruity
Christmas Ale
(5.3%), superbly
fruity-citrusy pale ale
India Pale Ale
(6.3%), sharply,
deliciously hopped
with Cascades

CATAMOUNT BREWING

Originally located in White River Junction, Vermont, close to the Ivy League's Dartmouth University, Catamount was Vermont's first commercial brewery since 1893. Named after the state's indigenous "catamount" mountain lions, the company was founded by a home-brewing physical education teacher, Steve Mason, at a time when micros just were reaching the east coast. In 1997, to cope with increasing demand, Catamount moved into a purpose-built brewery downriver in Windsor, transferring the yeast from the original brewery via canoe!

In addition to the IPA (originally a "Special Edition" 10th Anniversary brew) and particularly drinkable Porter – one of the earliest American examples to "nail" the style – Catamount offers two other year-round beers: an English-inspired Pale Ale hopped with Kent Goldings and Fuggles, and a balanced Amber where spicy hops meet sweetly nutty malt.

RIGHT: *It's function over form inside the Catamount brewhouse.*

Coined around 1664, catamount is short-hand slang for "cat-a-mountain" and denotes any of the various large wild cats.

All are well made examples of their respective styles. Seasonals include late winter's silky, biscuity Oatmeal Stout, an Oktoberfest lager, an extremely nutty-malty spring Bock, and summer's filtered American Wheat. An annual Christmas Ale, while perhaps not quite matching the IPA, balances a rich toasty malt character with loads of citrusy hops. Catamount's original Gold, clean-tasting and tangy-hoppy, is occasionally brewed.

Distribution is strongest in "lower" New England and the mid-Atlantic states. The company's growth has been steady, with production reaching around 20,000 barrels (23,500hl) in 1998.

RIGHT: *Catamount's bottles snake onto a pallet – then to consumers' palates.*

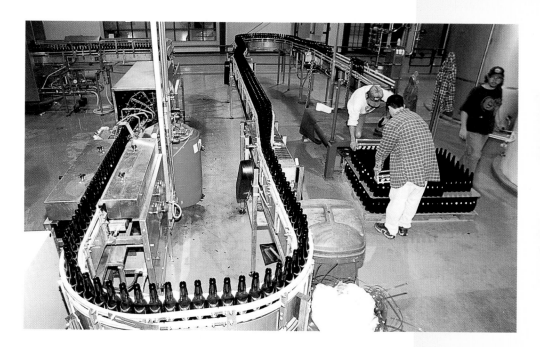

EST. 1986

38 Evergreen Drive,
Portland,
Maine 04103
Tel: (207) 878 2337

RECOMMENDED
Hampshire
Special Ale
(7%), assertively
hopped,
richly fruity,
toasty-malty

D.L. GEARY BREWING

This pioneering micro is in the "other" Portland. Assisted by the late founder of Scotland's Traquair House brewery, former medical-equipment salesman David Geary apprenticed at several small British breweries. Returning home, he opened his own small plant – one of the earliest in America built with the help of Peter Austin & Partners. It was the first commercial brewery in Maine for over a century.

Geary's flagship Pale Ale is cop-per-colored and dry, with four hop varieties (Cascade, Mt. Hood, Tettnang, and Fuggles) balancing its fruity character. The deep-brown, dry London Porter would partner better with the Maine lobster depicted on both its and the Pale's label. A crisper, American Ale, brewed with Oregon-grown Fuggles and Goldings hops, is a recent addition to the year-round line. Geary's first hot-weather beer, the pleasantly-fruity (but surprisingly potent) draft-only Summer Ale, was released in 1998. Its counterpart, the limited-season Hampshire Special Ale is (according to the brewery) "only available while the weather sucks" – which in Maine apparently means October through April. This classic wintertime strong ale has a powerful fruity character (that Ringwood yeast at work!) balanced with substantial helpings of English hops. Bottle-aging

will emphasize its rich, warming character.

Unlike many other eastern craft-brewers, Geary's has always been focused on its core market. This has meant slow, reliable growth and a granite-solid reputation with notably conservative Mainers (although Geary himself is nothing but, judging by his firebrand comments at industry functions). Production topped 15,000 barrels (17,600hl) in 1998.

Like its sibling city in Oregon, Maine's Portland also hosts many watering holes offering regional craft-brews.

41

IPSWICH BREWING COMPANY

EST. 1992
25 Hayward Street,
Ipswich,
Massachusetts 01938
Tel: (978) 356 3329

RECOMMENDED
Dark Ale
(6.4%), molasses
cookies and
earthy hops
Oatmeal Stout
(6.9%), massive,
but impeccably
balanced and
smooth

Founder Paul Sylva has two sailboats. One is his Aeolus, which he sails along the east coast as far south as the Caribbean. The other is on the label of his Ipswich ales. It's hard to say of which one he's more proud, but even landlubbers can appreciate the boldly plotted course of the beer. Distribution encompasses Massachusetts to New Jersey, with production topping 7,000 barrels (8,200hl) in 1997.

"Flagship" is an especially apt term for hoppy Ipswich Original Ale, the leader of the line. It is followed by the malty Dark Ale, massive Oatmeal Stout, fragrant IPA (hopped with Galenas, English Kent Goldings, Cascades), robust Porter, complex ESB, and quaffable Nut Brown. Two winter seasonals are offered: Winter Welcome is the draft powerhouse, while "1084 Barleywine" comes beautifully packaged in small clear-glass bottles. Ipswich also bottles their non-alcoholic Great American

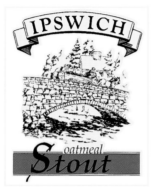

Root Beer. During 1998, some kegs and bottles of the IPA, Nut Brown, and ESB were contract-brewed at Clipper City in Baltimore, Maryland. This arrangement is no longer active.

Dedicated drinkers know not to worry about the quality of the Ipswich beers that are packaged in 64-ounce (1.88-liter) jugs. Although they give the impression of being hand-sealed in some brewpub backroom, the jugs are filled at the brewery by a fascinating, specially-adapted, automated Italian counterpressure system. Even with 12-ounce (354 ml) bottles of Ipswich readily available, the jugs still make up 60 percent of the brewery's bottle sales.

43

LOWELL BREWING COMPANY

EST. 1994
199 Cabot Street,
Lowell,
Massachusetts 01854
Tel: (978) 937 1200

RECOMMENDED:
Oatmeal Stout
(4.2%), molasses
cookies and coffee
Spindle Porter
(4.6%), a walk
on the malty side

Lowell, Massachusetts was the birthplace of the American Industrial Revolution. Lowell found fame as a mill town, where a precipitous drop of the Merrimack River was harnessed to power large textile mills. Lowell Brewing Company stands in one of the dormitories built for female mill workers; the site is over 160 years old

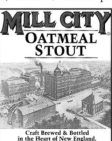

Craft Brewed & Bottled
in the Heart of New England.

and still solid as a rock. In addition to the brewery, the building houses a night club, sports bar, restaurant, and a "pub cinema" where patrons can enjoy their beer while watching a big-screen movie.

Lowell Brewing Company is also known to lovers of fine beers as the Mill City Brewing Company. Mill City's Boarding House

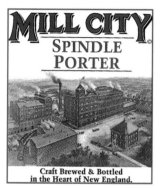

MILL CITY
SPINDLE PORTER

Craft Brewed & Bottled
in the Heart of New England.

Ale and IPA have fans, but true love is reserved for the chewy Oatmeal Stout and soothingly malty Spindle Porter (named for the waterpower transmission spindle in the old mills). Massachusetts winters are warmed by Mill City's Old Nutcracker seasonal, a strong ale with a toasted malt character. The brewery also has introduced an unabashedly mainstream American beer, Harvard Lager, which revives an old Lowell brewery name. Although beer purists may make unfavorable comparisons with the nearby river, its straightforward character could be just what's needed to keep the overall Lowell Brewing weaving ahead.

Too much internal tasting? Lowell's launch of "Harvard" lager promptly drew a lawsuit from the eponymous university.

MASS. BAY BREWING

★

EST. 1987
Harpoon Brewery,
306 Northern
Avenue,
Boston,
Massachusetts 02210
Tel: (617) 574 9551

**RECOMMENDED
Harpoon India
Pale Ale**
(5%), refreshing
Cascade-hopped
brew

Mass. Bay was founded by three business school graduates who had studied the prospects for a new beer company as part of their course—making it the "textbook" micro start-up, perhaps? The company's Boston brewhouse has been expanded steadily to cope with increasing production, nearing its 60,000 barrel (70,400hl) capacity

in 1998. Contracted production (bottles) from New York's F.X. Matt is used to buffer against "peaks" in demand.

Mass. Bay's original Harpoon Ale has been supplemented by a much broader year-round range that

RIGHT: *It takes a sharp brewer to navigate the tight, crowded Harpoon Brewery.*

includes the India Pale Ale, an ale-brewed Munich Dark, a German-themed Alt, and a Pilsner. Both the IPA and Alt began life as summer seasonals before entering the standard range. Current limited-season Harpoon brews include Spring Maibock, summertime's Snakebite (a cidery blend) and Summer ESB (a "quaffing-weight" example), a traditional Octoberfest lager, and spiced Winter Warmer.

Although its beers now are available throughout the northeast and mid-Atlantic (and even Florida), the company remains locally focused. It attracts Boston beer fans, for example, by hosting brewery parties on Oktoberfest and St. Patrick's Day, as well as a summertime "Brewstock." It also offers a free-ride shuttle service in downtown Boston that emphasizes

responsible drinking (i.e., not driving). The result of these activities
is something of a city-wide loyalty
to Mass. Bay's beers. Then again,
given the town's whaling history,
any sensible Bostonian would
rather stick with a Harpoon
than be stuck by one.

RIGHT: *In they go! A moment of drama
as one Harpoon brewer tips a bucket of
hop pellets into a kettle full of bubbling,
boiling wort.*

49

OTTER CREEK BREWING

★

EST. 1991
85 Exchange Street,
Middlebury,
Vermont 05753
Tel: (802) 388 0727

RECOMMENDED
Copper Ale
(5.85%),
well-balanced
toasty malt
flavor

Founded by a former home brewer who attended college in Portland, Oregon, the micro-brewing capital of America, Otter Creek actually began production with equipment purchased from Portland's Widmer Brothers Brewing! Middlebury was chosen as the brewery site because of its "relaxed" quality of life atmosphere and excellent quality brewing water. Expansion has been rapid and mainly locally-driven – especially when the brewery, at its start, offered only kegs of its flagship Copper Ale. Bottling commenced in 1993, pushing production even higher. In 1995, the company completed construction of a new purpose-built brewery with a capacity of 40,000 barrels (47,000 hl) per year. Otter Creek Brewing distributes

RIGHT: *Enjoying a tipple or two straight from the cask in Otter Creek Brewing's dedicated tour bar area.*

around the northeast.

Otter Creek Copper Ale, inspired by German altbiers, is brewed with five malts, roasted barley, and American-grown Hallertau and Tettnang hops. It has a solid copper color with smooth toasty-malt flavors and a pleasant background bitterness. It is offered year-round along with the brewery's Pale Ale, a pleasantly "different" beer dry-hopped with Cascades, and

deep, dark Stovepipe Porter. Five seasonals include a sweetish, chocolatey Mud Bock Spring Ale, effervescent Summer Wheat Ale, and moderately warming A Winter's Ale for the cooler months (and Shakespeare fans). Fall's Hickory Switch Smoked Amber Ale is not quite as much of a mouthful as its name suggests, and shares the season with an Oktoberfest ale.

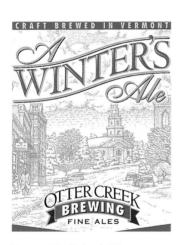

RIGHT: *Worth the wait! Lawrence Miller looks up to a pint of his finished product, Otter Creek Copper Ale.*

53

EST. 1993
43 Mechanic Street,
Camden,
Maine 04843
Tel: (207) 797 4022

RECOMMENDED
Windjammer
Blonde Ale
(5%), surprisingly
hoppy and firmly
fruity
Oktoberfest
(5.2%), a deserving
gold-medal winner
Jubilator
Doppelbock
(7.4%), lusciously
malty, rich

SEA DOG BREWING

Another brewpub that grew up. The Sea Dog first barked from a brewery pub on the western shore of Penobscot Bay in the historic shipbuilding town of Camden. It later took a bigger bite of the craft-beer market by building a larger production brewery (and adjoining pub) in Bangor, Maine. (In 1998, Sea Dog

sold its Bangor facility to Maine neighbor Shipyard.) The brewery first captured national attention when its traditional Oktoberfest captured top honors in its category at the 1994 Great American Beer Festival.

In addition to the seasonal Oktoberfest, Sea Dog also offers a Saaz-hopped Pilsner

throughout the year. Specialty lagers like its Jubilator Dopplebock and exuberant, spicy Maibock occasionally make appearances at the Camden pub. But Sea Dog's main focus for kegged distribution – throughout New England – is its core range of year-round ales. In addition to Windjammer, which is one of the most character-ful American golden ales, the company offers Old Gollywobbler Brown Ale and Old East India Pale Ale. The Brown drinks toasty and pleasantly hoppy, while the IPA (a hefty 7.5% and reportedly conditioned in oak barrels) at its best can be strongly fruity and seriously peppery-hoppy to match. A Hazelnut Porter, actually flavored with hazelnuts, also is produced, along with seasonal blueberry- and cherry-flavored wheat beers. Cabin Fever Stock Ale, a distinctly big-bodied winter warmer, was introduced in 1997.

EST. 1992
86 Newbury Street
Portland,
Maine 04101
Tel: (207) 761 0807

RECOMMENDED
Longfellow
Winter Ale
(5.5%), distinct
roasted barley
character
Old Thumper
(5.6%), huge,
complex fruit with
balancing
bitterness

SHIPYARD BREWERIES

This enterprise was established in 1992 as a brewery (Kennebunkport Brewing, #8 Western Avenue, 04043) in Kennebunk, Maine. A second "Shipyard Brewery" opened in 1994 in Portland, Maine, close to both the city's historic shipyard and the birthplace of famous poet Henry Wadsworth Longfellow. In 1995, the company entered an alliance with Miller Brewing (Miller purchased 50 percent of Shipyard Breweries). The deal, similar to that between Miller and the Celis Brewery (see page 188), has helped Shipyard capture attention (and shelf space) across the east coast and into the Midwest.

To love Shipyard's beers is to love the Ringwood yeast strain. Alan Pugsley, wandering brewmaster for Peter Austin & Partners, helped set up Shipyard's facilities and later became part-owner. The flagship Shipyard Export Ale (something of a Canadian-styled brew) clearly dis-

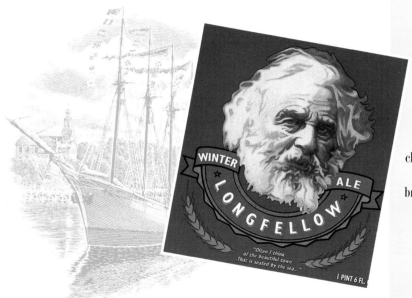

WINTER ALE

LONGFELLOW

"Often I think
of the beautiful town
That is seated by the sea..."

1 PINT 6 FL.

If Longfellow had inspired a champagne house instead of a brewery, we might see "Poet et Chandon."

Shipyard has been at the forefront of U.S. breweries' experiments with true "cask-conditioned" ales, as well as nitrogen dispense.

plays the signature Ringwood fruitiness. So does the company's pitch-black Blue Fin Stout and Mystic Seaport Pale Ale – although both, perhaps, are better balanced. Old Thumper, brewed to an "original" recipe from England's Ringwood Brewery, offers the best blend of complex fruit, toasty malt, and firm hop character.

Shipyard also offers specialties such as winter's Longfellow and a hearty holiday-season Prelude

Ale. Relatively new introductions include the "hop-onymous" Fuggles IPA, laced with that hop variety's flavor and aroma, and Chamberlain Pale Ale, a Maine-only beer named for the hero of the 20th Maine Regiment's defense of Little Round Top at Gettysburg. With so many choices, drinkers are likely to find at least one Ship(yard) they enjoy sinking.

EST. 1994
225 Heritage Ave.,
Portsmouth,
New Hampshire
03801
Tel: (603) 436 4026

RECOMMENDED
Old Brown Dog
(5.6%), a richly malty
brown ale
Imperial Stout
(7.1%), black, bitter,
burnt, beautiful

SMUTTYNOSE BREWING

★

Smuttynose Brewing Company is named for Smuttynose Island, one of the Isles of Shoals which lie nine miles (14 km) off the New Hampshire coast. The island has a colorful history: the pirate Blackbeard marooned his last wife there, for example, and it's where Louis Wagner (the last person executed in Maine)

committed his gruesome axe murders. Where better to build a brewery?

Actually, the brewery stands on the mainland coast, just outside Portsmouth. Smuttynose bought the facility of the failed Frank Jones brewery, an earlier micro that was good at brewing but bad at business. "We're very much aware

of the ghost of Frank Jones," brewery president Peter Egelston says with a wry grin. Egelston comes with experience; he and his partners run the successful Northampton Brewery in western Massachusetts.

The anchor of Smuttynose's line is Shoals Pale Ale, a smooth (buttery) American-style pale ale. Old Brown Dog is warming and comfortable, a malty quaffer. New in 1998 is Portsmouth Lager, roughly in the Dortmunder style and nicely rounded. Smuttynose has also started a series of "Big Beers" in 22 oz. bottles; a soft and fruity Barley Wine, a malty, lively Maibock, and the more assertive Imperial Stout. "I don't care if we make money on them or not," Egelston explains. "The idea is to gain visibility ... and notoriety." Just doing their part to maintain the Smuttynose image.

A "shoal," derived from the Old English word for shallow, refers to a sandbank or sandbar that affects water depth.

Also worth trying

The Northeast bursts with small brewers. Always check to see what's available locally when traveling in the region, and scan regional beer publications for local brewpubs. Vermont hosts perhaps the most colorful northeast micro, **McNeill's Brewery** of Brattleboro (love those tie-die T-shirts!), which offers bottles throughout Vermont and Massachusetts. Look particularly for McNeill's IPA, which has a fresh-hop aroma and balanced toasty-malt flavor. Burlington's **Vermont Pub & Brewery** – run by former industry-darling Greg Noonan, who also operates the **Seven Barrel Brewery** in Lebanon, Vermont – offers specialties such as Smoked Porter and a smooth, balanced Vermont Maple Ale. Burlington is also home to the psychedelic-styling **Magic Hat** brewery: the Blind Faith IPA will blow your mind, man. Hikers are rumored to find Bridgewater's **Long Trail Ales** (especially the hoppy, dry Double Bag Ale) suitably refreshing. As befits its thirst-inducing name, Plymouth's **Salt Ash Inn** brewpub serves a uniformly excellent array of beers.

Neighboring New Hampshire hosts its share

of brewers, including an Anheuser-Busch plant in Merrimack (which produces many of that company's specialty beers) and the eastern outpost of Seattle-headquartered Redhook in Portsmouth. **Nutfield Brewing** of Derry attracted attention in 1995 when elder American statesman Bob Dole sampled its golden Old Man Ale. **Martha's Exchange** brewpub, in historic downtown Nashua, offers a wide range of traditional styles: try the German-inspired HefeWeiss or Untouchable Scotch Ale. Nashua's **Skyview Cafe** is a new but already notable brewpub, having caber-tossed

its Kiltie's Pride Strong Scotch Ale into the ring. Celebrate your present good fortune with Lucknow IPA from **Castle Springs** in Moultonborough.

Massachusetts provides many stops for the beer lover. If you can't drink your fill at the popular Boston Brewers Festival (held in early summer each year), head for one of the city's several brewpubs – **Commonwealth Brewery** and **Boston Beer Works** (opposite Fenway Park) are the best. In nearby Cambridge, you can "pahk youah cahr by Hahvahd Yahd" and visit the original **John Harvard's Brewhouse**, which now

63

operates outposts in Atlanta and other eastern cities. The roof-deck beer garden at **Northampton**'s eponymous brewery – operated by the same team behind Smuttynose – offers a top spot to sample flagship Northampton Pale Ale and Black Cat Stout. **Dornbush Brewing** (contracting production at Ipswich) gets good reviews for its traditional Alt. **Hystand Brewing** brews a dramatically-hopped Amber Ale at its small facility in a large orchard outside Sturbridge; an upcoming IPA promises to stand even higher on the hoppy scale.

To the south, Rhode Island runs on brewpubs: capital Providence offers both the tiny **Union Station Brewery** (start with the clean, balanced Golden Spike Pale Ale) and newer **Trinity Brewhouse** (ask for India Point IPA, powerful and dry-hopped). You will also find cask ale from Kingston's **Emerald Isle Brew Works** in Providence; the Bank Street Bitter is fruity and refreshing. In Connecticut, the **Hartford Brewery** brewpub is expanding on the strength of beers like lagship Arch Amber and Bacchus Old Ale. **Hammer & Nail** pounds out a silky, molasses-touched Brown Ale in Watertown. Norwalk's **New England Brewing** already offers bottles and kegs throughout the region. Its "steam-style" Atlantic Amber and generously-hopped (Perle, Northern Brewer, Cascade, Saaz) Gold Stock Ale roll out of a gorgeous brewery and pub, featuring a Bavarian-built brewhouse, in the city's historic south end.

Finally, far northeastern Maine holds over 30 brewers. Portland offers the famous **Gritty McDuff's** brewpub, **Stone Coast Brewing** and **Casco Bay Brewing**. Visit Portland's Great Lost Bear pub (540 Forest Avenue) for the top selection of draft northeast brews. The tiny **Andrew's Brewing** of Lincolnville offers a delicious Porter and other brews under its "Andy's" label. **Bray's Brewpub** in Naples serves up Old Church Pale Ale: a communion of hops, fruit, and dry maltiness. Bar Harbor offers two brewpubs – **Atlantic Brewing**, with its acclaimed Coal Porter, and Maine Coast Brewing – as well as micro **Bar Harbor Brewing** (try the Thunder Hole Ale and Cadillac Mountain Stout). **Sunday River Brewing** of Bethel, whose owners also operate Portland's Stone Coast, greets patrons at one of the east coast's premier ski areas. Bi-coastal travelers should try blending Sunday River's Black Bear Porter with California's Golden Bear Lager for an ursine (if slightly ersatz) Black & Tan!

MID-ATLANTIC

The "Mid-Atlantic" states, from New York down to northern Virginia, have a proud brewing tradition that stretches back into the earliest Colonial times. Unfortunately, even once-mighty brewing capitals such as Philadelphia (home to more than 100 breweries in the late 1800s) and New York City (host of Schaeffer, Rheingold, and other legendary brands) fell prey to post-Prohibition consolidation.

The first micros moved in during the 1980s, inspired by west coast pioneers, and many more recently have arrived. In general, Mid-Atlantic craft brews divide evenly between ales and lagers.

The former tend to have English accents that may reflect the region's early history. The latter testify to its life as a destination for central European immigrants (America's first commercial lager beer was brewed in Philadelphia).

Bi-monthly "brewspapers" keep tabs on the Mid-Atlantic's dynamic brewpub and beer scene. *BarleyCorn* (P.O. Box 549, Frederick, Maryland 21705) offers in-depth regional coverage, while *Ale Street News* (P.O. Box 1125, Maywood, New Jersey 07607) also reports on the northeast. *The Malt Advocate*, a glossy devoted to beer and whisk(e)y, is published quarterly out of Pennsylvania (3416 Oak Hill Rd., Emmaus, 18049).

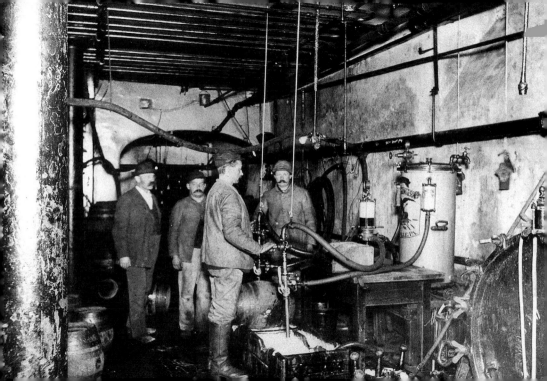

EST. 1989
104 Albemarle Street,
Baltimore,
Maryland 21202
Tel: (410) 837 5000

RECOMMENDED
DeGroen's Pils
(5.3%), a good
everyday quaff
Rauchbock
(6.7%), a "robusto"
of a smoked beer
Doppelbock
(8.5%), fat, round,
and sweet

BALTIMORE BREWING COMPANY

★

Theo DeGroen has two advanced degrees that have shaped his life. He is a graduate of Weihenstephan, the premier German brewing school, holding its five-year degree of Brewing Engineer. He also holds an MBA from Duke University. While he was completing his MBA he noted the rise of the western micros and conceived the idea

of the Baltimore Brewing Company. He opened his brewpub in 1989 on the site of a former Baltimore brewery.

From the start, DeGroen's beers have been German lagers and weizens. It's what he knows best, and it's part of the city's immigrant brewing heritage (Baltimore-based writer H.L. Mencken often commented on the quality of local beers). Playing up his German themes, DeGroen has instituted "tapping celebrations" to mark the release of his popular Maibock and Oktoberfest lager.

For years only available at the brewpub and on draft across town, DeGroen's beers are now bottled for off-premise sales. The bottled range includes the year-round flagship Märzen, dark and smooth Dunkles, and zesty Pils – a firm Bohemian-styled brew. Certain seasonals such as the big, tangy Rauchbock, slyly strong Doppelbock, well-muscled Maibock, and summer's quaffing Helles also make it into bottles. DeGroen's hoppy Altfest, frothy Weizen, and powerfully good Weizenbock remain draft only. Another good reason for visiting the brewpub (besides seeing if Mencken's comments still hold true).

EST. 1988
118 N. 11th Street,
Brooklyn,
New York 11211
Tel: (718) 486 7422

RECOMMENDED
Brooklyn Lager
(5.2%), refreshing,
hoppy amber brew
**Black Chocolate
Stout**
(8.2%), smooth,
rich, seductive
Imperial

BROOKLYN BREWERY

★

Brooklyn was founded by a banker and an Associated Press correspondent (who discovered that brewing was more enjoyable than dodging bullets on his Middle East assignment). Their original Brooklyn Lager was designed in the style of a "pre-Prohibition beer" by a retired east coast brewmaster who once worked for Rheingold; it remains the brewery

flagship, widely available across New York City. Brooklyn later brought aboard its highly-regarded current brewmaster, Garrett Oliver.

Under Oliver's guidance, Brooklyn reformulated its chocolatey Brown Ale and also launched two seasonals, Black Chocolate Stout (winter) and a powerfully hoppy East India Pale Ale (now year-round). The extremely positive reception to these gutsy brews was a clear sign that New York's beer scene finally had "come of age." More recent introductions include Brooklyn Pennant Pale Ale, a solidly toasty brew, and Brooklyn Pilsner, noble-hopped in the Germanic tradition.

While the majority of Brooklyn's beer is contract-brewed at F.X. Matt and 10 Springs Brewing – the Saratoga Springs facility built by the failed Nor'Wester Brewing and now associated with Mendocino – the company opened a small pub and draft-only brewery in its home borough in 1995. Barrels of Brooklyner Weiss (Bavarian-style hefeweizen), Blanche de Brooklyn (witbier-style), the Monster of Brooklyn barley wine, and a Belgian dubbel-style Abbaye de Breukelen flow from this new Brooklyn Brewery. Across the street are the company's offices, from where it also runs New York's best specialty-beer distributorship.

Nothing if not creative, Brooklyn's Oliver once cooled a fermenting tank by continually running water down its outside.

71

★

EST. 1995
4615 Hollins
Ferry Road, Suite B,
Baltimore,
Maryland 21227
Tel: (410) 247 7822

RECOMMENDED
**Chesapeake
Amber**
(4.8%), aromatic
and mellow in
English style
**Chesapeake
Reserve Maibock**
(6.5%), full-bodied,
malty, hints of
melon

B altimore's "biggest microbrew-ery" opened to the great antici-pation of craft-brew lovers in late 1995. Founder Hugh Sisson is famous around the city's beer scene, having lobbied the state to legalize brewpubs before promptly opening the first, Sisson's, in 1989. His new brewery's name echoes Baltimore's status as a major seaport, once known for the tall clipper ships that plied the waters of nearby Chesapeake Bay.

Sisson's eponymous original brewing venture remains a heavily-trafficked fixture in the developing Batimore beer scene.

Clipper City also produces beer under contract for Ipswich Brewing of Massachusetts.

Sisson is building a small fleet of Clippers. Chesapeake Amber and Chesapeake Gold are the brewery's price-competitive beers, excellent for a summer night spent cracking Maryland crabs. The more distinctive Clipper Reserve line is led by the flagship Premium Lager, originally a mainstream-oriented beer but recently retooled as a Czech-style Pils. This "upgrade" speaks volumes about how Baltimore's tastes have evolved since Clipper City opened only a few years ago. It is joined seasonally by the malty, satisfying Maibock, a lip-smacking Honey Wheat Ale, stingingly crisp IPA, and Winter Ale, a supercharged version of the IPA.

The brewery continues to grow at a steady clip(per): production topped 5,000 barrels (5,850hl) in 1998. Distribution reaches throughout Maryland, Washington DC, and parts of Virginia.

EST. 1995
22 Nassau
Commons, Lewes,
Delaware 19958
Tel: (888) 8-DOGFISH

RECOMMENDED
Chicory Stout
(5.2%), rich yet
drinkable, smooth
coffee notes
Immort Ale
(11-12%), huge:
herbs, tobacco,
vanilla, and
smoke

DOGFISH HEAD CRAFT BREWERY

"Whoso would be a man must be a non-conformist." Sam Calagione steers Dogfish Head by the light of this Emerson quote. It has been a fiercely individualistic enterprise from the start, an attitude that clearly comes through in Dogfish Head's idiosyncratic beers.

Dogfish Head grew from a brewpub in nearby Rehoboth (320 Rehoboth Ave.) to their nearly hand-built micro in Lewes. After a quiet release of the malt-tilted Shelter Pale Ale, Dogfish Head decided, in the immortal words of *Spinal Tap*, to "go to eleven." Introduced at the end of 1995, Immort Ale shocked people with its exotic character and unwavering intensity. Pale and wheat malts, peat-smoked malt, maple syrup, juniper, vanilla beans, and brown sugar all

come together with a tag-team of yeasts and chipped oak from French Chardonnay barrels. After some months of aging, Immort Ale emerges malty, powerful, and shot through with marvelous layered aromas and tastes.

But nothing is small here. Chicory Stout is rich and chewy with coffee nuances (from organic Mexican beans) and has an addition of "nature's Prozac," St. John's wort.

The brewery's draft "Seasonales" include Raison d'Etre, brewed with kola nuts and raisins (get it?); High-Alpha Wheat, which mixes Bavarian weizen cloviness with lavender buds and a snootful of hops; and Winter Ale, a well-melded melange of sugars and spices. All in all, Dogfish Head is making Delaware (and other eastern areas) well aware of distinctive beer.

F.X. MATT BREWING

EST. 1888
811 Edward Street,
Utica,
New York 13502
Tel: (315) 732 3181

RECOMMENDED
Saranac Golden
(5.25%), refreshing,
dry-hopped lager
Saranac Pale Ale
(5.5%), balanced
and pleasantly
hoppy
**Saranac Chocolate
Amber**
(5.8%), robust
Munich-style
dunkel

With its attractive brick build-ings, huge copper kettles, and Victorian-style visitors' cen-ter, the F.X. Matt brewery would be right at home in the English countryside. Its origins, however, are totally Teutonic. After leaving his brewery in Germany's Black Forest region in 1878, Francis Xavier Matt plied his craft in upstate Utica (at the foothills of New York's Adirondack Mountains). There he offered both the region's traditional ales and his homeland's lagers. The brewery survived Prohibition by producing soft drinks, only to see sales decline as drinkers abandoned its

RIGHT: *A "Matt Pack" – up the creek with a paddle are family members Fred, F.X., and Nick (left to right).*

In the lean years before micros, F.X. Matt was one of only a few U.S. breweries to continue to make true ales.

Utica Club beers for new national brands.

During the 1980s, Matt began offering its services, experience, and excess capacity to the new generation of contract brewers. Their successes finally inspired brewery-head F.X. Matt II to launch his own craft-beer line under the Saranac label. As sales have grown, the Saranac range has expanded from its initial Amber lager to include a total of 14 beers, with some – such as the English-inspired, Kent Golding-hopped Pale Ale – more adventurous than others. Notable seasonals include fall's Stout (usually only blended into a popular Black & Tan), spring's complex Chocolate Amber, and a truly refreshing Summer Wheat in the witbier mold. Overall, Matt has reinvented itself more successfully than most other older American regionals.

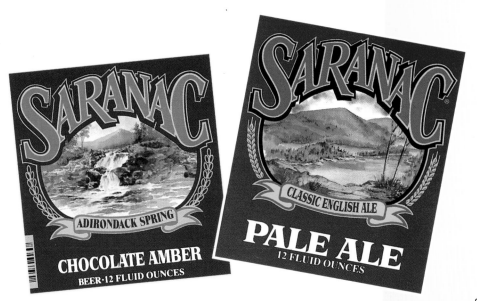

EST. 1996
18 Olney Ave.
Bldg 44,
Cherry Hill,
New Jersey 08003
Tel: (609) 489 0061

RECOMMENDED
ESB Ale
(5.5%), solid malt
character, strong
secondary bitterness
**Belgian Abbey
Dubbel**
(7.3%), big malty
body finishes
nicely dry

FLYING FISH

★

E xperienced, award-winning homebrewer Gene Muller needed a good name for his new commercial brewery – a brewery which, incidentally, he founded via the Internet and a website long before establishing the actual property. Flying Fish seemed irreverent and fun, he recalls. With the

creation of a striking logo (a fish-skeleton with propellers attached), Gene and company were in business.

But don't think Flying Fish is nothing more than a market-ing-driven operation. Gene's always looking for ways to stay ahead of the curve, and finds it in his versions of Belgian styles: a rich, drop-dead Dubbel, crisply refreshing Farm house Ale (in the saison style), and teasingly complex and tart Grand Cru. The latter is brewed from a sour mash of only Belgian Pilsner malt, augmented with a small amount of Belgian "candi" sugar. Cask-conditioned versions of most of the beers are offered to the brewery's top accounts.

The Flying Fish school also includes its dual flagships – ESB (brewed with imported Belgian malts) and XPA (eXtra Pale Ale, hopped with Fuggles and Mt. Hoods) – as well as a bottle-conditioned Porter. There also are rare sightings of Blackfish, a draft pre-mix of the Porter and XPA. With relatively broad availability in bottles and kegs across their home region, Flying Fish beers thankfully are easy to catch.

Is Flying Fish the *"reel"* deal? Consumers certainly seem *hooked*, tipping the *scales* towards greater *net* profits.

EST. 1993
4607 Wedgewood
Blvd.,
Frederick,
Maryland 21701
Tel: (888) 258 7434

RECOMMENDED
Blue Ridge HopFest
(varies), annual early
fall seasonal
Blue Ridge
Steeple Stout
(6%), deeply roasted,
smooth, intense
Wild Goose
Snow Goose
(6.2%), fruity,
complex, warming

FREDERICK BREWING

★

Frederick Brewing started small in this quiet Maryland town. But things change. Frederick outgrew their original brewery quickly and built a large (80,000 barrels/93,600hl annual capacity) new brewery nearby in spring 1997.

High times ensued when brewer Steve Nordahl dreamed up Hempen Ale, a light-bodied brown ale spiked with hemp seeds. The sterilized, imported seeds added a slightly spicy character and a creaminess to the ale – and put Frederick in the news nationwide. While the seeds contain none of the psychoactive element in hemp, they do have

RIGHT: *Inside a Frederick Brewing fermenting tank: the beer level rises – but is it getting high?*

hemp's notoriety — which boosted sales to the point that a second hemp beer, Hempen Gold, was added.

Frederick developed a case of "the munchies" after Hempen Ale. In early 1998, the company gobbled up two other Maryland brewers, tiny Brimstone and the larger, established Wild Goose. Brimstone will continue as a line of small-batch, large-character beers (like the wildly estery Big Strong Ale). Frederick has committed to maintaining the Wild Goose line, which includes a chocolatey Porter and rich, dark Oatmeal Stout. Winter's generously fruity Snow Goose, styled after an English old ale, will return annually.

Frederick also still brews their original Blue Ridge family of beers, notable for the rich, big-bodied Steeple Stout (brewed with a portion of flaked rye) and two seasonals, spring's Subliminator doppelbock and early fall's HopFest. HopFest uses one specific hop variety (different each year) to highlight an unfiltered American brown ale base. 1998's Ahtanum hop-spiced version left people smacking their lips and looking for more. But the usual small production run left them thirsty and ... hopping mad.

RIGHT: *Brimstone was acquired in 1998.*

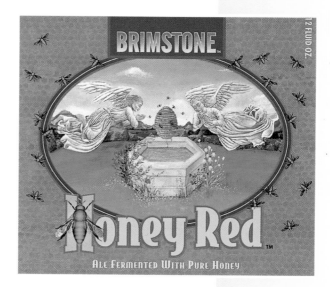

EST. 1990
44622 Guilford Drive,
Ashburn,
Virginia 22011
Tel: (703) 689 1225

RECOMMENDED
Dominion Stout
(4.7%), creamy,
complex, quaffable
**Tuppers' Hop
Pocket Ale**
(6%), pale, fruity, and
"extravagantly
hopped"
**Dominion
Millennium**
(10.4%), deliciously
chewy, fruity, and
hoppy

OLD DOMINION BREWING

Located outside of Washington DC, about three miles (5km) north of the capital's Dulles International Airport, Dominion quickly has become one of the country's most significant craft-brewers (producing 23,300 barrels/27,340hl in 1997). At the same time, its market remains relatively local (Virginia, DC, and parts of Maryland) – "steep and deep," as the saying goes. More than 20 different ales and lagers are brewed, some exclusively for restaurants and pubs in the region. Dominion also produces a root beer to an old recipe that founder Jerry Bailey (who formerly worked in the Federal Government's "foreign aid" office) researched at the Library of Congress.

While flagship beers such as Dominion Ale and Lager are pleasant, the brewery's abilities shine in Tuppers' Hop Pocket Ale (dry hopped with whole Mt. Hoods

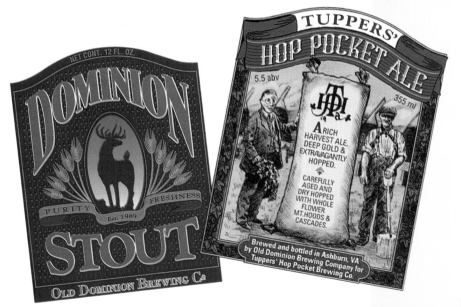

NET CONT. 12 FL. OZ.

DOMINION

PURITY   FRESHNESS

Est. 1989

STOUT

OLD DOMINION BREWING Cº

TUPPERS'

HOP POCKET ALE

5.5 abv

355 ml

A RICH
HARVEST ALE,
DEEP GOLD &
EXTRAVAGANTLY
HOPPED.

CAREFULLY
AGED AND
DRY HOPPED
WITH WHOLE
FLOWER
MT.HOODS &
CASCADES.

Brewed and bottled in Ashburn, VA
by Old Dominion Brewing Company for
Tuppers' Hop Pocket Brewing Co.

and Cascades) – actually a contract brew produced for a family associated with DC's famous Brickskeller bar. A second Tuppers' brew, the unfiltered Hop Pocket Pils, was introduced in 1997. Dominion's seasonal beers, especially the defiantly-peppery Saaz Bock (a kind of "super-Pils" released under the

Spring Brew label in bottles), also can be rewarding.

Most complex is Millennium, a now-annual barley wine – brewed to 100 bitterness units, dry hopped with English Kent Goldings (half a pound per barrel), and bottle conditioned– first brewed to celebrate the company's 1,000th batch of beer in 1993.

EST. 1997
New York Rt. 33,
Cooperstown,
New York 13326
Tel: (800) 656 1212

RECOMMENDED
Ommegang
(8.5%), an
authentic dubbel
brewed in
America

OMMEGANG BREWERY

T iny Cooperstown, New York, is nationally famous as the home of the Baseball Hall of Fame. But Cooperstown has added a new

landmark: the beautiful Ommegang, a Belgian-American brewery with a unique pedigree. This joint venture stemmed from the creative minds of Don Feinberg and Wendy Little-field, owners of Vanberg & DeWulf, a import company specializing in fine Belgian beers.

With the direct involvement

RIGHT: *The future looks bright for Ommegang's Belgian-style ales, produced at this Belgian-style "farmhouse" brewery.*

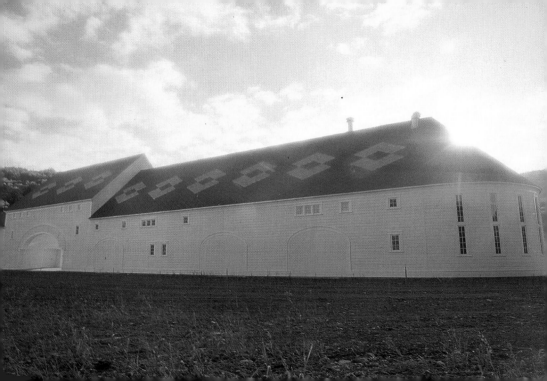

of the Belgian brewing families of Moortgat (brewers of Duvel), Dubuisson (Scaldis), and Vervloet (Affligem), Omme-gang hit the ground running, a brand-new brewery boasting 1,247 combined years of experience. The brewery uses traditional methods – tweaked slightly to suit the American market – to brew its bottle-conditioned, bottle-matured

Ommegang (a full-flavored dubbel) and Hennepin Ale (similar to a saison, with sharp grapefruit and fresh ginger character). The latter takes its name from the Belgian missionary who discovered Niagara Falls. A third "Brabant-style ale," Rare Vos, will join the lineup in 1999.

The beers were immediately successful, thanks to their quality and to Vanberg & DeWulf's established distribution network. The beautiful farmhouse brewery is humming as it runs flat-out to meet demand. But Ommegang promises it will properly mature every drop of beer, a promise supported by more than 12 hundred years of brewing tradition.

RIGHT: *A bold label for a beer yet unborn: packaging for Rare Vos was ready before the beer's final recipe*

EST. 1986
800 Vinial Street,
Pittsburgh,
Pennsylvania 15212
Tel: (412) 237 9400

RECOMMENDED
Dark
(5%), lots of caramel
notes, smooth
Oktoberfest
(5.6%), rich malt in
aroma and flavor
St. Nikolaus Bock
(8.4%), chewy,
chocolatey, with rich
caramel flavor

PENN BREWING

★

This German-inspired brewery was founded by Tom Pastorius, who spent 12 years working in Germany and is descended directly from the founder of America's first German settlement (Philadelphia's "Germantown"). The flagship Penn Pilsner was Pennsylvania's first craft beer (albeit produced under contract). In an effort to educate industrial Pittsburgh's "industrial beer" drinkers Pastorius opened his Penn Brewery brewpub in 1989. Its German-built, copper-vessel brewhouse and horizontal lagering tanks have been expanded to

RIGHT: *It's on a roll! Kaiser Pils and other specialties flow from Penn's classic-styled vessels.*

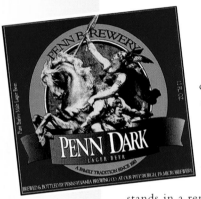

cope with growing demand (20,000 barrels/23,500hl in 1997). All Penn Brewery's draft beers come from this facility, which stands in a renovated section of Pittsburgh's old Eberhardt & Ober Brewery.

Penn Pilsner is joined in year-round bottles and kegs by the smooth Munich dunkel-style Penn Dark, an award-wining Munich-style Helles Gold, and a new unfiltered Weizen (Silver medal, 1997 Great American Beer Festival). Bottles of Penn Pilsner, along with some Penn Dark and Penn Gold, are produced under contract at old Pennsylvania regional Jones Brewing. Bottled seasonals include the highly-regarded Oktoberfest, and winter's potent St. Nikolaus Bock – guaranteed to make you jolly, if not old! The latter's label features a famous illustration of St. Nick drawn by Thomas Nast for Harper's Bazaar in 1881. Draft specialties include a Weizen Bock, a hoppy Kaiser Pils, smooth and soft Maibock, and a top-fermented Altbier. There's also an occasional Pastorator doppelbock, guaranteed to generate some German inspiration of your own!

RIGHT: *Today Penn Brewing occupies a tiny part of the former Eberhardt & Ober brewery in Pittsburgh.*

STOUDT'S BREWING

★

EST. 1987
Route 272,
P.O. Box 880,
Adamstown,
Pennsylvania 19501
Tel: (717) 484 4387

RECOMMENDED
Gold
(5%), the cleanly
malty flagship
Pils
(5%), solidly bal-
anced, classically
appealing
Honey Double
Mai Bock
(7.5%), big body,
creamy and
finessed flavor

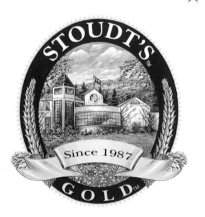

S toudt's brews seem to increase in flavor the closer one gets to the brewery in tiny Adamstown. The one place this beery theory doesn't hold true is Denver, where the beers have collected around 20 gold, silver, and bronze medals at the Great American Beer Festival. Still, there's no question that the brewery's on-site "Gemütlichkeit" – Stoudt's hosts many Bavarian-themed festivals and events – brings out the best in its brews.

Situated in Pennsylvania Dutch country, the brewery began as a natural outgrowth of the beer garden and restaurant operated by Carol and Ed Stoudt. All their original brews were lagers, a fact that distinguished Stoudt's from other early micros (most of whom made

RIGHT: *The brewhouse that bock built? Stoudt's crafts three varieties of the rich, strong lager style at its Adamstown home in Pennsylvania.*

Pennsylvania's "Dutch" country is a corruption of "Deutsch," referring to the area's many German settlers

ales). Although the Dortmunder Export-style Gold, with its firmly malty character, remains the brewery flagship, the Saaz-hopped Pils and three different bocks (Bock, Honey Double, and Honey Double Mai) have staunch fans. The brewery's range also now encompasses ales, including a Bavarian-style unfiltered Weizen, an English-inspired

ESB, a banana-fruity "abbey triple" and "abbey double"—and (yes, you've guessed it) Stoudt's stout.

All of Stoudt's beers are available unpasteurized in signature "champagne bottles" (765ml in capacity). Stoudt's also contracts 12oz. versions of some of their beers at The Lion brewery in Wilkes-Barre, Pennsylvania.

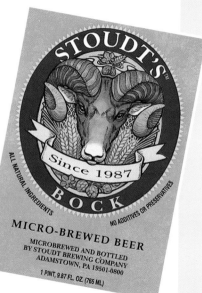

EST. 1996
420 Acorn Lane,
Downingtown,
Pennsylvania 19335
Tel: (610) 873 0881

RECOMMENDED
Prima Pils
(5.3%), heaps of
hops on a smooth
malt base
HopDevil IPA
(6.3%), nutty malt,
lots of tangy hop
Storm King
Imperial Stout
(9.1%), rich and
loaded with
fruity esters

VICTORY BREWING

★

Bready aromas have yielded to the fragrance of fermenting beer at this former Pepperidge Farm bakery, which once produced 77,000 loaves per week. Mid-Atlantic beer lovers watched with great expectation when Weihenstephan-trained Ron Barchet, former head brewer at Old Dominion, and Bill Covaleski, ex-assistant at Baltimore Brewing, opened their new micro and attached pub. The advanced 25-barrel (29hl) brewing system features integrated German designs for decoction-mashed lagers, a hopback

RIGHT: *A victory for metalworkers! Pipes, railings, decking, and more in the functional brewhouse.*

(where the flagship HopDevil India Pale Ale gets a final helping of whole-cone Cascades), and open fermenters for ales. In addition to the IPA, Victory's main range includes the briskly-hopped Prima Pils and a firmly malty Dortmunder named after the surrounding Brandywine Valley. A Bavarian-style Festbier is available year-round on draft, seasonally in bottles.

The year-round brews are excellent, but they are eclipsed by Victory's seasonals. These good things come in twos: winter's lightly smoky, velvety smooth St. Victorious Doppelbock (8.0%) and spring's St. Boisterous Hellerbock (7.5%); the Jekyll and Hyde combination of summer's Sunrise Weiss (5.2%) and fall's Moonglow

Weizenbock (8.0%); and the holiday one-two punch of Storm King and Old Horizontal Barleywine (11%). (Some aficionados like to lay down bottles of Old Horizontal to improve with age; others, after enjoying one or two, simply like to lay down). With big guns like these, Victory seems certain.

RIGHT: *Beer with "legs!" Bill Covaleski (left) and Ron Barchet come up shorts on the Victory brewdeck.*

EST. 1995
5050 Umbria Street,
Philadelphia,
Pennsylvania 19128
Tel: (215) 482 9109

RECOMMENDED
Entire Porter
(5.7%), traditionally
blended, chocolatey
and rich
ESA
(6.3%), lively, fruity,
enveloped in
Kent Goldings

YARDS BREWING

Like most state "alcohol control" bureaucracies, the Pennsylvania Liquor Control Board is generally humorless. At least some of the PLCB staff, however, must be amused to know that Yards Brewing occupies the leased back half of their Philadelphia warehouse. Yards took over the space in 1997, after outgrowing their tiny original location in the popular Manayunk neighborhood.

But the brewery has not out-grown their hometown market. Philadelphia continues to drink up almost all the production, to the point where Yards is hardly known (and seldom seen) 50 miles (80km) away. Yards ESA was one of Philly's first beers dispensed with hand-pumps as "real ale." The draft version offers a billowing cloud of hop aroma, courtesy of the "hop pocket" of whole-cone East Kent Goldings inserted in each keg.

Bottles of the flagship ESA (dry-hopped in the tank) have been available since 1997, with all the other Yards beers available only on draft. Brawler is a feisty nitrogen-dispense bitter with hops enough to punch through its creamy head. Entire Porter returns to the roots of this historic British style, made by blending a dark mild ale with a bold Imperial stout (occasionally released on draft by itself). There is also a smartly-spiced, somewhat Belgian-style Saison for the summer, an occasional "Old Peculier-ish" Old Ale, a wintertime Old Bart barleywine with sweet golden heft, and an annual Valentine's Day edition of Love Stout – an oyster stout brewed with "shells and all" (the whole nine Yards?).

The name Yards arose out of a search for a "classic English" moniker – a contraction of Scotland Yard, rumor has it.

109

EST. 1829
5th & Manhantongo
Streets,
Pottsville,
Pennsylvania 17901
Tel: (717) 622 1094

RECOMMENDED
Porter
(4.7%), actually
a balanced
dark lager

YUENGLING BREWING

★

America's oldest operating brewery, founded by German immigrant David Yuengling (pronounced "ying-ling") in the mining town of Pottsville (108 miles/174km northeast of Philadelphia). The current brewery buildings, raised in 1831, stand on a steep hillside where tunnels were bored into the rock to take advantage of natural cool temperatures for fermentation and lagering.

By the late 1800s, Yuengling's beers had won such a following that the company constructed additional breweries in Virginia, New York

RIGHT: *A nostalgic look at Yuengling's keg-racking cellars in the days of ye olde bushy moustaches.*

> Several years ago, Yuengling tangled with (and triumphed over) Anheuser-Busch in a lawsuit about its eagle logo.

state, and Canada. But Prohibition brought expansion to a halt. Like many old regionals, Yuengling survived (by producing low-alcohol "near beer") only to see even its loyal local market – where customers refer to the beer as "Vitamin Y" – systematically eroded by national brands.

The brewery has reclaimed its success under fifth-generation Dick Yuengling Jr. His approach involved introducing new brews, like a popular Black & Tan and Yuengling Traditional Lager, and repositioning old ones (Lord Chesterfield Ale, Yuengling Premium Beer) to emphasize history and tradition. Regional demand rebounded so substantially that, in 1998, Yuengling ran out of room for on-site expansion. To supply its thirsty consumers, Yuengling is building a new 1.5 million barrel brewery a mile away from the current brewery. The "old" location will remain in operation after the new one opens.

Yuengling originally produced both lagers and ales: signs in its on-site museum tout a "Brilliant Ale" and "Brown Stout." Today's beers, despite their names, are all lagers. Each offers a taste of American brewing history, but the chocolatey Porter (effectively a Munich-style dark) is the most distinctive.

RIGHT: *Tradition sells: Yuengling's "old style" packaging is a modern twist to enhance consumer appeal.*

Also worth trying

After a decade of cold-shouldering micros, New York City now is awash. High-profile spots like d.b.a. (41 First Avenue) feature rarities such as the whopping Braveheart Scottish Ale from upstate's **Woodstock Brewing**. Among the brew-pubs, Manhattan's **Heartland Brewery** and Brooklyn's **Park Slope Brewing** get top reviews, and the failed Zip City Brewing has metamorphosed into **The Tap Room** (brewing lager beer in a building which once housed the National Temperance Society). Strike out

upstate to visit **Cooperstown Brewing** (Old Slugger Ale is as crisp as the crack of ball on bat), **Empire**'s two noteworthy brewpubs in Syracuse and Rochester, and **Ellicottville Brewing** (try the wonderfully fruity Porter). **Mountain Valley**, on the New Jersey border in Suffern, bottles their distinctive beers; the Ruffian Porter is suitably robust.

In "Joisey" itself, you'll find clean beers and great German food at the **Long Valley** brewpub. Butler's **High Point** specializes in Bavarian-style wheats, while Princeton's **Triumph Brewing** offers

an education in well-made ales and lagers for a fraction of tuition at the nearby university. New Brunswick's Old Bay Restaurant (61 Church Street) is one of the country's premier beer spots.

In Philadelphia, draft Belgian beers are showcased alongside micros at center city's Monk's Cafe (264 South 16th Street). Philly brewers include **Red Bell** (a deliciously deep Wee Heavy) and **Independence** – a more mainstream micro but for small "secret" runs of beers like Anniversary Bock – whose name seems ironic in light of a potential buy-out by regional Pittsburgh Brewing. **Poor Henry**'s is a micro/pub combo where Henry Ortlieb, scion of one of the city's oldest brewing families, now makes the Dock Street brands as well as his own spitfire of an IPA. Moving upstate, **Lancaster Malt Brewing** and **Weyerbacher** (in Easton) hold down the brewpub fort. The Pocono Mountains are well-watered by **Franconia** (an all-German micro; lagers, alt, weizens). Harrisburg's **Troegs Brewing** pours a beautiful ESB. Despite its Erie location, there's nothing spooky about **Hoppers** brewpub and its Scotch Ale-inspired Railbender.

115

Heading south? Don't forget Delaware! Newark's **Iron Hill** brewpub is worth at stop for their Lodestone Lager. Baltimore beer-lovers flock to bars on Fells Point for **Oxford Brewing**'s Special Old Bitter. Feeling sporty at Camden Yards? Walk to the nearby **Wharf Rat** brewpub for a glass of Oliver's Ironman IPA (Oliver's Ales are now showing up in bottles, too). Uptown, the **Brewer's Art** brewpub serves Belgian-styled brews. Around Washington DC, Gaithersburg's suburban **Olde Towne Tavern** and Arlington's funked-up **Bardo Rodeo** offer completely different brew-pub experiences. For local suds, head to the capital's Big Hunt (1345 Connecticut Avenue NW) or Brickskeller (1523 22nd Street NW), arguably the best bottled-beer bar in America.

In Virginia, look for the great fruity-n-hoppy Mobjack Bay Pale Ale or Rappahannock Red Ale (named for DC's other river). The long-lamented Virginia Native has been reborn as **Southern Beverage**, making a malt-layered Virginia Native Dark lager. There's also a growing host of smaller producers that are worth looking out for, such as Richmond's **Legend** (a luscious chocolatey Porter) and **Williamsville Brewing** (the provocatively fruity Man Go Ale).

SOUTHEAST

Maybe it's the Bible belt's religious beliefs and "dry counties," where no alcoholic beverages can be sold. Maybe it's the ridiculous beer laws in some states that outlaw brews above 6% alcohol (but do nothing to stop the sale of rotgut liquor or cheap fortified wines). Whatever the reason, America's Southeast – that curved swath of states from North Carolina through Louisiana – has been slow to embrace craft-brewing.

The movement largely has been carried by brewpubs, which have done much to wean drinkers away from "mainstream" American suds. The resulting proliferation of craft beers in a few areas, particularly Atlanta, is an encouraging sign that southern tastes are turning to flavorful, full-bodied brews. So is the success of micros such as Louisiana's Abita Brewing and North Carolina's Highland Brewing. Southerners thankfully are beginning to appreciate the same distinctiveness in beer that they enjoy in much of their region's food and drink: from Louisiana's spicy crayfish-boils to Kentucky's single-batch bourbons.

Southern Draft Brew News – Southeast Edition (1346 Bridgeson Court, Norcross, Georgia 30093) is the region's colorful brewspaper. The national *All About Beer* magazine is headquartered in North Carolina (1627 Marion Ave., Durham, 27705).

ABITA BREWING

EST. 1986
P.O. Box 762,
Abita Springs,
Louisiana 70420
Tel: (800) 737 2311

RECOMMENDED
Bock
(6.1%), smooth,
sweet spring
seasonal
Turbo Dog
(6.1%), deep
chocolate-
brown ale

Fresh brew from the Bayou? Close enough. Abita Springs stands in the piney woods across Lake Pontchartrain from New Orleans. Since its early days as a Choctaw Indian settlement, visitors have come to sample the town's "restorative" artesian spring water. This untreated water, drawn from a 2,000-foot (610m) well, today provides the soul of Abita Brewing's lagers and ales. Despite some rough going in its early days, Abita now ranks among the country's larger craft-brewers (producing 34,000 barrels/39,900hl in 1997). It also enjoys a popular cult following

RIGHT: *Reinheitsgebot, Schmeinheitsgebot! Sweetening the mix at Abita, hopefully for root beer.*

throughout the South.

The flagship Abita Amber and Golden, both refreshing lagers, sell well in the humid region – as does the Purple Haze, a raspberry wheat beer. Turbo Dog, a brown ale produced year-round with Amber and Golden, is more complex and rewarding. Same goes for limited-season beers such as Abita Bock, Fallfest, and the dark Christmas Ale (brewed to a different recipe each year). The seasonal brews also include a clean-tasting Wheat lager and Red Ale. Distribution reaches across the Southeast, Texas, and select markets along the east coast and in the Midwest.

Abita showcases its brands at its brewpub (72011 Holly Street), a charming place at least as worthy of a pilgrimage as the famous springs.

RIGHT: *Bottling line thoughts: "Label straight? Check. Code readable? Check. Am I wearing one funky hat? Check."*

EST. 1995

201 N. Carrollton,
New Orleans,
Louisiana 70119
Tel: (504) 483 9003

RECOMMENDED
Pilsener
(4.6%), malty
with a crisp,
bitter finish
Helles Bock
(6%), rich
and malty,
well balanced

ACADIAN BREWING

Find Acadian Brewing nestled in the Big Easy and you've discovered a little bit of Germany. Brewery founder Jim Cronin and head brewer Doug Lindley have helped Acadian make its niche in the local specialty beer market by brewing German-style lagers.

Acadian and its adjacent tap room (dubbed

"The Beer Garden") stand in a former marine shop with ceilings high enough to accommodate boat masts. Lindley keeps a crucifix perched above the brewhouse because German brewers traditionally believe that such an icon protects the beer. The fact that vampire-story author Anne Rice is a local surely has nothing to do with it ....

Acadian's dedication to German-style beers was rewarded early on, when Lindley was invited to brew a Pilsener for the 1996 National Homebrewers Conference staged in New Orleans. The result was the forerunner of today's flagship Acadian Pils – a glowing example of the German style fortified with a decent dose of Saaz hops. Acadian also bottles its Hallertau-hopped Vienna Amber, a notably well-balanced lager in that style. The company brews draft-only beers for sale at the Beer Garden (and in limited distribution): Hefe-Pils is an unfiltered version of Acadian's Pilsener, while Helles Bock is brewed using a triple decoction mash for a smooth, sweet, yet balanced flavor.

The Big Easy got its name because people there like to take their time; Lindley is no exception. It's not uncommon for beers like Helles Bock to condition for a whopping six months before release.

EST. 1993
1219 Williams Street,
Atlanta,
Georgia 30309
Tel: (404) 892 4436

RECOMMENDED
Summer Brew
(4.5%), citrusy, floral,
with a dry finish
Red Brick Ale
(5.7%), coppery-red,
malty depth,
slightly sweet
Winter Brew
(5.9%), dark,
delicately spiced with
Curaçao, ginger

ATLANTA BREWING

★

Atlanta's oldest operating brewery was founded when Greg Kelly, a marketing veteran from Guinness, dreamed of drinking fresh craft beer in this southern hub. The brewery, located in Atlanta's "midtown" district, occupies a red brick building that was a warehouse for a printing company – hence the name of its flagship Red Brick Ale. Production reached about 10,000 barrels (11,735hl) in 1997 with distribution primarily throughout Atlanta and north Georgia.

Following a trend started by the Northwest's Redhook and Widmer breweries, Atlanta Brewing has entered an "alliance" with

LEFT: *Greg Kelly, founder of Atlanta Brewing, hoists his flagship Red Brick Ale.*

Anheuser-Busch. The agreement endowed Atlanta Brewing with the powerful distribution, marketing, and financial resources of Anheuser-Busch, in return for giving the St. Louis brewer (and Redhook) about a 25 percent interest in the craft brewery in the form of future stock options. If this arrangement has had any effect on Atlanta Brewing's beers, it actually seems to have made them better.

Three brews are offered year-round: Red Brick Ale, Red Brick Golden Lager, and Laughing Skull Bohemian Pilsner (subdued, but pleasantly drinkable). Laughing Skull's ghostly name and image are used under license from The Vortex, a popular Atlanta haunt familiar to local beer drinkers. Atlanta Brewing also offers two seasonals: Winter

Brew and Summer Brew, the latter of which is dry-hopped with the relatively new Ahtanum variety.

Atlanta Brewing's beer recipes have undergone several changes over the years, but the company seems to have finally settled on some winners. As a result, the brewery is a major force in Atlanta's specialty-beer boom.

RIGHT: *In the Atlanta Brewing brewhouse; specific gravity is checked with an instrument called a hydrometer.*

EST. 1992
3118 3rd Avenue S.,
Birmingham,
Alabama 35233
Tel: (205) 326 6677

RECOMMENDED
**Red Mountain
Red Ale**
(4.8%), notable
nutty-malt flavor
**Vulcan Hefe
Weizen**
(4.8%), unfiltered,
refreshing;
banana and
clove aromas

BIRMINGHAM/VULCAN BREWING

Prohibition came early to Alabama in 1908, forcing the original Birmingham Brewing Company to dump 300 barrels of fresh beer into the streets. Thankfully, no such misfortune has befallen the brewery's new incarnation: it remains Alabama's oldest (!) and largest brewery, as well as the state's only bottling brewery. Birmingham's flagship brand is Red Mountain Red Ale, an English-style brown ale that picked up a medal at the 1995 Great American Beer Festival. Medium-bodied and quaffable, it displays hints of citrus and berry-fruit flavors over its malty base.

In 1996, Birmingham Brewing was purchased by Vulcan Breweries, Inc. The new company's name refers not to Mr. Spock of *Star Trek*, but rather to the Roman god of fire

131

and metalworking – a reference to a bygone era when Birmingham teemed with steel mills. A second line of beers now is produced under the Vulcan Brewing Company label: the ethereal Vulcan Hefe Weizen is a fine example of the Bavarian style (it collected a bronze medal at the 1997 Great American Beer Festival). Still, the company's easy-drinking brews reveal where local tastes fall on the beer learning curve.

In an effort to refocus on its home market, Vulcan pulled back the distribution of Birmingham Brewing's beers to the surrounding metro area. Now brewery officials have set their sights on Atlanta, Nashville, and Mobile as expansion markets for 1999. It remains to be seen if, under Vulcan's leadership, the overall company will live long and prosper.

EST. 1994
42 Biltmore Avenue,
Asheville,
North Carolina
28801
Tel: (828) 255 8240

RECOMMENDED
Black Mocha Stout
(5.3%), roasty,
chocolate notes and
smoky finish
Gaelic Ale
(5.8%), delicately
hopped, rich
and malty
Oatmeal Porter
(5.9%), chocolate
flavors with well-
balanced hoppiness

HIGHLAND BREWING

It's unclear which aspect of Highland Brewing is more remarkable: that it crafts a solid portfolio of Scottish-style ales in the basement of Barley's Taproom (a popular Asheville beer bar housed in a renovated, historic building); or that all its beers are brewed and fermented in former dairy tanks that were scavenged from across western North Carolina.

But the colorful character of the operation doesn't end there.

Highland cooks up beer for its neighboring restaurant, the Blue Rooster Brewhouse, and then pumps it some 20 feet (6m), through a wall, into three 35-barrel fermentation tanks that stand behind the Blue Rooster's bar. As a result, the Rooster is better dubbed a "ferment-pub" rather than a brewpub, as its beer is not actually brewed on the premises.

The first craft brewery in this scenic mountain town, Highland offers four year-round beers. Besides

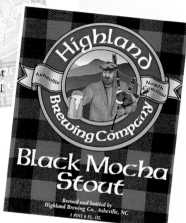

the flagship Gaelic Ale and Oatmeal Porter (a robust classic), two newer brews are worth tasting: Kashmir IPA, a brilliant dry example with an aggressive hop character, and St. Terese's Pale Ale, a crisp, refreshing ale with a delicate dry-hop aroma. Highland also makes three seasonals: late fall's Black Mocha Stout (which may enter the year-round range), spring's Scotch Ale (less a "wee heavy" than a potent 80-Shilling style, brewed with peated malt), and September's Highlandfest (which is a traditional Oktoberfest beer).

Production reached roughly 3,000 barrels (3,500hl) in 1997, but the brewery expects that figure to double as it switches from 22-ounce bottles to standard 12-ounce bottles. Distribution encompasses the Carolinas, north Georgia, and eastern Tennessee.

135

NEW KNOXVILLE BREWING

EST. 1996

708 E. Depot
Avenue,
Knoxville,
Tennessee 37917

Tel: (423) 521 7870

RECOMMENDED
Mild Ale
(3.5%), session beer,
light malty finish
Porter
(5.2%), chocolate
hints, slight
bittersweet finish
India Pale Ale
(5.6%), dry and crisp
start, hoppy finish

Prohibition also came early to Tennessee, in 1907. A few years later, the state government discovered that Swanky Temperance Brew, a "non-alcoholic" beer from the original New Knoxville Brewing, actually did contain alcohol. The brewery was shut down and its charter revoked. More than 80 years later, Ed Vendely, a former banker, flies the company's flag again at his English-style ale brewery in the city's Old Town district. Vendely's passion for good beer developed a few years earlier when he owned a homebrew supply shop in nearby Oak Ridge. True to English tradition, New Knoxville employs open fermentation tanks, which are used in only quite a small percentage of today's craft-breweries.

Faring no better than its predecessor, the revived New Knoxville's Swanky English Ale never proved popular and has been discontinued. The Porter, however, is another story –

supposedly a recreation of the style as brewed in the 1890s by the original New Knoxville. Deep reddish-black in color, with a rich malty flavor, it is one of the modern brewery's most popular brews. Indeed, many Volunteers have stepped up to drink it in this University of Tennessee town. At the other end of the flavor spectrum, New Knoxville's medium-bodied, English-inspired IPA will satisfy hopheads.

The brewery also offers seasonals such as summertime's Honey Wheat, a light-bodied golden ale (with a hint of sweetness from Tennessee wildflower honey), and winter's draft-only Stout (a complex dry Irish stout). The year-round Mild Ale is an enjoyable example of this rarely-seen subdued style; worth celebrating even though there's nothing "swanky" about it!

EST. 1997
900 Wendell Court,
Atlanta,
Georgia 30336
Tel: (404) 691 2537

RECOMMENDED
Sweetwater Ale
(5.0%), well-
balanced,
pleasantly-hopped
amber ale
Exodus Porter
(5.6%), unfiltered,
with rich chocolate
character

SWEETWATER BREWING

The trio of Sweetwater partners chose to build their start-up brewery in Atlanta because the city is the nexus of the South-east — a region that was lagging behind the rest of the country in its craft-brewery popul-ation. Their plan seems to be paying off. In the brewery's first year, flagship Sweetwater Ale

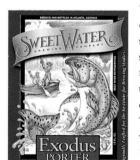

received a silver medal at Denver's Great American Beer Festival (in the "English-style bitter" category). Sweetwater subsequently was selected by the Institute for Brewing Studies to make a special commemorative "Symposium" beer when Atlanta hosted the 1998 National Craft-Brewers Conference.

In mid-1997, Sweetwater introduced its crisp, clean 420 Extra Pale Ale. Enjoyable and refreshing, it is a slightly-light interpretation of the classic "west coast pale" style. Rumors immediately began circulating that "420" refers to the presence of "controlled substances" such as marijuana in the beer, but the partners maintain that the name comes from the date of the first brew (April 20th).

Sweetwater's year-round portfolio also includes the smooth Exodus Porter – developed as the Symposium Porter in 1998 – and Sweetwater Blue, a light-bodied ale brewed with pale and wheat malts and fresh blueberries. Festive Ale, for the holiday season, is reminiscent in style of a spiced old ale.

Sweetwater beers are distributed throughout the Atlanta metropolitan area as well as in Athens, Georgia. The brewery produced around 5,000 barrels (5,850hl) in 1998.

Atlanta's 1998 Craft-Brewer Conference featured a keynote address from Anchor Brewing's Fritz Maytag on the joys of "staying small."

139

EST. 1994
2205 North 20th
Street,
Tampa,
Florida 33605
Tel: (813) 242 9222

RECOMMENDED
Gaspar's Ale
(5.2%), malty with
notable hop
bitterness

YBOR CITY BREWING

★

Tampa's Ybor City (pronounced "ee-boor") neighborhood is something like the French Quarter of New Orleans. It was once a vibrant ethnic district rich in cultural traditions. It also once hosted a number of small breweries, the last of which closed in the early 1960s. Recent redevelopment has helped Ybor City reclaim its colorful past; Humberto Perez is helping reclaim its brewing traditions. Born to a brewing family in Venezuela, Perez is the former president of Cerveceria Regional (brewer of that country's second biggest-selling beer). Attracted to America by the booming micro market, and to Tampa by its Venezuelan-like climate, he settled on Ybor City for his site. But his "perfect location" already had a

If you take a six-pack of Ybor City's pirate brew golfing, does it count as "Gaspar for the course?"

building on it – so Perez spent $2.6 million on the purchase and renovation of the 100-year-old Seidenberg & Co. cigar factory, which had stood dormant for 25 years.

Ybor City's flagship Ybor Gold is a quenching golden lager brewed for Florida's tropical thirsts. The real star in Ybor's portfolio is Gaspar's Ale, a balanced porter with notes of chocolate and coffee. This seasonal was originally brewed for Tampa's Gasparilla Festival, staged in February, but is now available from December through March. Gasparilla (both the beer's and the festival's namesake) was a pirate – perhaps "buccaneer" is a better word, given the locale – of Spanish descent based around Tampa Bay in the early 1800s.

Other Ybor City offerings include the year-round Calusa Wheat (a light American-style version) and the distinctive Ybor Brown (English-inspired, mellow).

Also worth trying

North Carolina has hopped on the micro-brew bandwagon. A smoky Black Radish lager comes from the first brewpub established in the Southeast: **Weeping Radish Brewery** in Manteo, on the Outer Banks. The Raleigh-Durham area bodes well for beer research: Chapel Hill's **Carolina Brewery** offers a supremely hoppy IPA and roasty Old North State Stout, while **Carolina Brewing** (of Holly Springs) presents a Pale Ale with lots of fresh hop flavor. Durham's **Top of the Hill** brew-pub has the backing of *All About Beer* magazine's

publisher, Daniel Bradford.

In Florida, **Miami Brewing**'s vice was discontinuing its Hurricane Reef Amber Ale; now it rolls out a quaffable Caribbean Pilsener and new line of specialty styles, launched with an Oktoberfest. Lager-lovers in New Orleans should visit resurrected regional **Dixie Brewing**, which promotes the craft-beer spirit with its Blackened Voodoo Lager. Meanwhile, the Tennessee-based Big River group attracts attention for its cask ales at a trio of brewpub concepts – including **Big Rivers** in Nashville and Chattanooga, as well as Florida's Disney World Epcot Boardwalk – in five states throughout the Southeast.

Separated from Cincinnati by the Ohio River, **Oldenberg Brewing** in Kentucky – which is opening brewpubs in a few southern states – is famous for "Beer Camp," a three-day extravaganza (staged each March and September) of seminars, discussions, and activities that draw beer enthusiasts from across North America. Talk about happy campers.... Meanwhile, **Lexington Brewing** produces Kentucky Hemp Beer, a Pilsner-style brewed with hemp seeds. It makes happy campers even happier.

Until recently, brewpubs remained illegal in several southern states. The Bible belt thankfully has loosened....

145

MIDWEST

America's "heartland" is also the center of its brewing industry. With Anheuser-Busch in St. Louis, Miller in Milwaukee, and Stroh in Detroit, the nation's first-, second-, and fourth-largest brewers all are headquartered in the Midwest. And although they have introduced a few specialties – from Michelob Pale Ale to Stroh's Weinhard's Hazelnut Stout – the Big Boys still churn out millions of barrels of mainstream lagers.

The Midwest's taste for lager beer originated in the waves of central and northern European immigration that flooded the region during the 1800s. German and Scandinavian settlers demanded the beers of their homelands – bocks, dunkels, weizenbiers, and more. Even as bland industrial beers claimed greater market shares, these classic styles were not forgotten. Nor were all the regional breweries that once produced them. Today, the Midwest remains a bastion of imported German brews, from rich doppelbocks to classic wheat beers *mit hefe*.

As a result, the region offers both great opportunity and challenge for microbrewers. Education is needed to overcome decades of devotion to American megabrands, but the Midwest's thirst for traditional German beer styles allows the introduction of brews (such as hefeweizens) that elsewhere are a harder sell. Micros finally appear to be reaching critical mass – even in Chicago, where a wheeler-dealer beer trade still favors the nationals. Read *Midwest Beer Notes* (P.O. Box 237, Ridgeland, Wisconsin 54763) and *Great Lakes Brewing News* (214 Muegel Road, East Amherst, New York 14051) to keep abreast.

AUGUST SCHELL BREWING

EST. 1860
Schell's Park,
P.O. Box 128,
New Ulm,
Minnesota 56073
Tel: (507) 354 5528

RECOMMENDED
Pils
(5.6%), refreshingly
hoppy from
imported Hallertau
Maifest
(6.9%), smoothly
drinkable
spring bock

A regional brewery that battled back from the brink of collapse through new emphasis on specialty beers (both its own and brands it makes under contract). The company is still owned by descendants of German immigrant August Schell, who have maintained close ties with the sur- rounding area for over a century. (In 1862, when native American Indians torched much of New Ulm during the Dakota Uprising, they spared the brewery because of friendship

RIGHT: *The five-acre estate gardens at August Schell welcome not only beer fans but also deer and peacocks.*

with the Schells). Known regionally for mainstream lagers, the brewery first attracted national notice with its long-produced Bock (perhaps the best available example of the old "American" style).

An alliance with beer pioneer Charles Finkel prompted the introduction of Schell's hoppy German-style Pils and filtered Bavarian-style Weizen in 1985. The success of these brands spawned others, such as spring's balanced, refreshing Maifest (a "blonde double bock"). A candy-ish DoppelBock also is offered. The German-themed company even has ventured into ales – first with its chocolatey Schmaltz's Alt (an "alt-porter"?), then with a hybrid "German Pale Ale." Other seasonals include an Octoberfest lager and Blizzard Ale. When in New Ulm, the cognoscenti tour Schell's five-acre gardens and deer park (also populated by several peacocks), which adjoin the original brick brewery buildings. While there, don't forget to visit Schell's Museum of Brewing for a nostalgic journey into the early days of the industry in America.

151

BOULEVARD BREWING

EST. 1989
2501 Southwest
Boulevard,
Kansas City,
Missouri 64108
Tel: (816) 474 7095

RECOMMENDED
Dry Stout
(5%), a smooth
quaffer, dispensed
with nitrogen
Bully! Porter
(5.5%), well-made
hoppy, roasty version
Nutcracker Ale
(5.9%), holiday
seasonal with
molasses and spicy
Chinook hops

Billing itself as "Missouri's second largest brewery" (behind St. Louis juggernaut Anheuser-Busch), Boulevard Brewing stands in a turn-of-the-century warehouse originally built as a laundry for the Santa Fe Railroad. The company was founded by John McDonald, a former carpenter who dis-

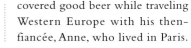

covered good beer while traveling Western Europe with his then-fiancée, Anne, who lived in Paris.

The brewhouse came second-hand from Brauerei Vierkirche, a small brewery situated in Germany.

Boulevard brews five year-round beers (including a buttery Irish Ale and the draft-only stout) and

Bob's '47 is Boulevard's most popular seasonal, selling out so quickly that it has cult status among area beer lovers

HELLO! FROM

BOULEVARD

KANSAS CITY,

It turns out that "New York strip" is just a gussied-up name for a cut of beef that originated as a "Kansas City strip."

three seasonals (winter's Nutcracker is unfiltered for extra character). The flagship Boulevard Pale Ale displays a fruity, well-hopped character, while the Porter offers an enticing blend of hop character (dry hopped?) and rich, roasty malt. Fall sees the arrival of Boulevard's one and only true lager, Bob's '47, whose recipe originated at New York's now defunct U.S. Brewers' Academy and was passed on to Boulevard by the late master brewer Bob Werkowitch (a 1947 graduate of the Academy).

Boulevard confines its sales to nine central plains states and intends to keep its focus concentrated on the Midwest region. With projected sales for 1998 at 35,000 barrels (41,000hl), Boulevard surely is on the road to success.

Pale Ale

BOULEVARD
BREWING CO.
™

12 fl. oz.

Boulevard's flavorful Pale Ale is hand-crafted in a
style once popular in America. Brewed with tradition
ingredients: water, two row barley malt, hops and ye

Our Unfiltered

BOULEVARD
BREWING CO.®

Winter Warmer

NUT
CRACKER
ALE

BOULEVARD   KANSAS CITY MISSOURI ™   BREWING CO.

EST. 1986
7734 Terrace
Avenue,
Middleton,
Wisconsin 53562
Tel: (608) 836 7100

RECOMMENDED
Garten Bräu Special
(4.9%), hoppy
German-styled
Pilsner
Garten Bräu
Doppelbock
(7.5%), big,
sweetish,
chocolatey

CAPITAL BREWING

★

C apital is a craft-brewer dedicated to making the Midwest's favored German beers. Much of its equipment, including twin copper brewing vessels, came from Germany's Hoxter Brewery. The Garten Bräu name comes, appropriately, from an on-site beer garden whose fencing is covered with hops and grape vines: open to families, it offers a slice of Bavarian life to complement the fresh German-style brews. Capital offers more than 15 beers throughout the year, between its regular range and

RIGHT: Brewmaster Kirby Nelson keeps a watchful eye on the progress of Capital's latest batch of beer.

It takes a lot of drive to microbrew in Wisconsin, the state that made American beer infamous.

BLONDE DOPPELBOCK

WISCONSIN BEER   GERMAN STYLE

12 FLUID OUNCES

CAPITAL BREWERY

special or seasonal brews. Production in 1997 reached 14,000 barrels (16,400hl) and distribution includes nine Midwestern states and a few east coast outposts.

The top-selling Special testifies to the region's taste for both classic German imports and mainstream golden lagers. Its well-made character is echoed by Garten Bräu Dark, a balanced example in the Munich style. The year-round range also includes a Bavarian-style Kloster (hefe)Weizen, English-inspired Brown Ale, Vienna-styled Wisconsin raspberry wheat ("The Razz"). Seasonals, including Capital's potent Doppelbock, are perhaps more interesting. Both a springtime Maibock and autumn Oktoberfest (as well as the just-plain Fest) are worthy of celebration. Garten Bräu Wild Rice is made with Wisconsin-grown "grain" (actually a grass) which imparts a complex, spicy character.

EST. 1988
1800 West Fulton,
Chicago,
Illinois 60612
Tel: (312) 226 1119

RECOMMENDED
Summertime
(4.5%), refreshing,
well-made, with
subtle complexity
India Pale Ale
(5.9%), spicy-lemony
hops over rich malt
**Bourbon County
Stout**
(11.5%), truly
unique and
deliciously whiskyish

GOOSE ISLAND BEER COMPANY

A famous "Second City" beer-maker, named after an island in the Chicago River. The original large, comfortable brewpub (1800 North Clybourn) was supplemented in 1995 with a full production craft-brewery (funded in part through ties with the Beer Across America microbrew-of-the-month club). Expanded capacity allows distribution throughout Chicago and the Midwest. The brewpub still offers more than 30 well-crafted, rotating styles – everything from a "starter" Blonde Ale to a Dunkelweizenbock and Finnish-inspired Sahti.

In addition to Goose Island's flagship Honkers Ale, a balanced pale ale hopped with Styrian Goldings, a variety of ales are available in bottles and barrels from the new site. The year-round IPA boasts hefty bittering

(65 BUs) to balance its rich malt base; its dark counterpart is a mellow Oatmeal Stout. Seasonals include spring's Kilgubbin Red Ale – "Kilgubbin" is Gaelic for Goose Island, once home to Irish settlers – and Summertime (a Kölsch) and winter's Christmas Ale (brewed with Belgian malts).

Draft specialties at the pub have included Demolition 1800 Ale (a potent Duvel-styled brew) and Bourbon County Stout. The latter is made by aging a powerful stout for a minimum of 100 days in ex-Jim Beam Bourbon barrels. Extremely complex and surprisingly drinkable, it fortifies well against the "Windy City" weather.

In 1997, Goose Island acquired the Baderbräu label from failed micro Pavichevich Brewing Co. of Elmhurst, Illinois. Now Goose Island produces Baderbräu's Lager (a Vienna-style version) and Pilsner (Czech Saaz-hopped, quite quaffable).

EST. 1988
2516 Market Avenue,
Cleveland,
Ohio 44113
Tel: (216) 771 4404

RECOMMENDED
Dortmunder Gold
(5.8%), deep golden,
firmly balanced
Burning River
Pale Ale
(6%), bags of
refreshing citric
hop character
The Eliot Ness
(6.2%), malty,
spicy, well-made
Vienna lager

GREAT LAKES BREWING

Great Lakes opened as a brewpub in an 1860s building where industrialist John D. Rockefeller once worked. Subsequent expansions included an outdoor beer garden and a full-production micro in an adjacent building. Between this new brewery and the original (which still makes specialties like "Loch Erie" Scotch Ale), production topped 12,000 barrels (14,000hl) in 1997. Distribution is strongest in the Midwest and South, including Tennessee and Kentucky.

In 1997, Great Lakes began renovating a turn-of-the-century brewery — conveniently located

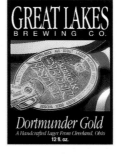

RIGHT: *Pat and Daniel Conway alongside a great big Great Lakes "gold medal" bottle.*

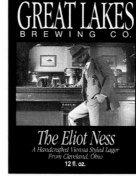

The Eliot Ness
A Handcrafted Vienna Styled Lager
From Cleveland, Ohio
12 fl. oz.

Burning River Pale Ale is named for an infamous incident when Cleveland's then-polluted river caught on fire.

right next door to its original brewery – in the Cleveland's Ohio City neighborhood. The old Schlather Brewing Co. will soon house Great Lakes' new 75-barrel brewery, which ultimately will be able to craft 100,000 barrels (117,340hl) per year.

Brewery flagship Dortmunder Gold is a medal-winning example of that lager style. Burning River Pale Ale is deliciously fruity and fresh-tasting; one of the best in America. Eliot Ness, brewed with Hallertau and Tettnang hops, is well-made (if not untouchable) in the Vienna style. Seasonals include a chocolatey-malty Rockefeller Bock ("as rich as its name"), a thoroughly hoppy Commodore Perry IPA, and Christmas Ale flavored with honey, cinnamon, and ginger.

Springtime's Conway's Irish Ale,

named after the grandfather of owners Pat and Daniel Conway, has a strongly malty aroma and rich toasty-malt flavor balanced by peppery Kent Golding hops. Its deep character illustrates why many consider Great Lakes to be the Midwest's greatest micro.

RIGHT: *Part of the Great Lakes brewery and pub complex on Market Avenue. The outdoor beer garden helps Clevelanders celebrate the arrival of summer.*

167

EST. 1985
355 E. Kalamazoo
Avenue,
Kalamazoo,
Michigan 49007
Tel: (616) 382 2338

RECOMMENDED
Bell's Amber Ale
(5.5%), softly fruity
and hoppy
**Bell's Kalamazoo
Stout**
(6.5%), roasty, rich
with molasses hints
Third Coast Old Ale
(10.2%), deliciously
thick, chewy
barley wine

KALAMAZOO BREWING

Attention beer lovers: ask not for whom the Bell toils ... he toils (and boils) for thee! The personality of Kalamazoo founder Larry Bell is best described by the name of his brewery's on-site Eccentric Cafe. Bell vacillates between shunning publicity and staging colorful stunts to get it: for example,

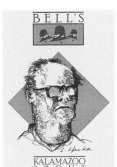

he once produced a provocative television commercial for the brewery that showed a German-themed accordionist deliberately shattering his instrument and setting it ablaze! Brewing occurs on an assortment of systems, including Bell's "sacred" original 15-gallon (57-liter) soup kettle. Production neared

Third Coast Old Ale

CA CASH REFUND

BELL'S

AMBER ALE

"Third Coast" refers to the vast waterfront of Michigan and the other Great Lakes border states.

20,000 barrels (23,500hl) in 1998, and distribution encompasses the upper Midwest and the area of greater Chicago.

The flagship Bell's Amber is joined year-round by a firm Pale Ale, a lightly-roasted Porter, a gentle Third Coast Beer, and a robust Kalamazoo Stout. The year splits between three "seasonals" – Oberon Ale (a buttery American wheat) in summer and Best Brown Ale (as well as über-hopped Two Hearted Ale) in winter. But it is the specialty brews, that are offered in limited quantities throughout the year, that draw the most attention. These include an intensely rich Expedition Stout (11.5%), the fruity but balanced Cherry Stout, and warming Third Coast Old Ale. Many additional specialties are only available at the brewery cafe. All the company's beers are unfiltered, unpasteurized, and naturally carbonated.

Two Hearted Ale

BELL'S

PALE ALE

EST. 1987
1872 North
Commerce Street,
Milwaukee,
Wisconsin 53212
Tel: (414) 372 8800

RECOMMENDED
Riverwest
Stein Beer
(6%), nutty amber
lager with "crisp"
hops
Holiday Spice
(9%), billowy-spicy
and extremely well
balanced

LAKEFRONT BREWING

Another brewery which again joins grain and yeast in a former bakery build-ing. The founding Klisch brothers (one is a police detective) built much of their plant from used equip-ment. "I call it my Frankenstein," jokes Russ Klisch about the jumbled facility, "because almost every

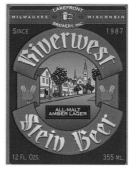

piece previously has lived, died, and been resurrected here." To enhance aesthetics, three fermenting tanks are painted with the heads of Larry, Curly, and Moe of the Three Stooges.

Despite its piecemeal appearance, Lakefront produces seriously distinctive beers. The flagship Riverwest

173

Stein Beer – not a Rauchenfels-type stone beer, but rather named for a drinking "stein" – is clean, quaffable, and crisply hoppy thanks to Mt. Hoods and Cascades. Other year-round brews include Lakefront Cream City Pale Ale (fruity, drinkable), East Side Dark (a strong dunkel), and Klisch Pilsner (generously hopped with Mt. Hoods). The honey-fortified Holiday

Spice – which matures well in the bottle – caps off a range of rotating seasonals such as fall's famous Lakefront Pumpkin Beer, a late-winter Cherry Beer, spring Bock, and sweetish summertime Weiss (Bavarian style). Specialties have included an organic ESB, a robust coffee stout, and an unfiltered "Beer Line" barleywine designed to age in the bottle.

NEW GLARUS BREWING

★

EST. 1993
P.O. Box 759,
New Glarus,
Wisconsin 53574
Tel: (608) 527 5850

RECOMMENDED
Apple Ale
(4.8%), deliciously
cider-like in character
**Wisconsin
Belgian Red**
(5%), fantastically
flavorful Belgian-
style kriek
Snowshoe Ale
(5.7%), hoppy, fruity,
darkly malty

176

This small micro makes some of the best fruit beers in America, if not the world. It was founded by Daniel and Deborah Carey in a Swiss-settled town near Wisconsin capital Madison. Daniel previously worked for brewery-installation company J.V. Northwest, and ultimately rose to the role of production supervisor at Anheuser-Busch's Fort Collins plant. His experience seems to be paying off: 1998 saw New Glarus build a

3,000 square-feet (280m²) expansion to house a new, gleaming copper brewhouse and a gift shop.

New Glarus offers five year-round beers: the soft Edel Pils, dark chocolatey Uff-Da Bock, unfiltered Spotted Cow "farmhouse ale," award-winning Wisconsin Belgian Red Ale, and a truly fruity

RIGHT: *Carey-ing on! Dan and Deb show off the US-made brew that has inspired an international following.*

Apple Ale. The latter, a wheat-based brown ale blended with Cortland, MacIntosh, and Jonathon apples (squeezed at a nearby orchard), has an out-standing fresh "farm cider" flavor.

The justly-famous Wisconsin Belgian Red is brewed with aged Willamette hops and more than a pound of whole local Wisconsin cherries per 750ml bottle. It is based on a Flanders-style sour brown ale – think Liefmans Kriek, but a little sweeter – and surely is one of the most distinctive beers to emerge from America's modern brewing renaissance.

New Glarus also produces a range

of eight limited-season beers including: early spring's sweetish Coffee Stout; late spring's Cabin Fever, a Belgian-style triple with a heady bouquet; the new Raspberry Tart, a framboise-style wheat ale (made with aged Hallertau hops); and the wintertime Snowshoe Ale, billed as an authentic Irish Ale.

RIGHT: *Talk about "heavy medal!" Awards for New Glarus' Belgian Red keep coming in, to the brewer's delight.*

EST. 1986
2264 University
Avenue,
St Paul,
Minnesota 55114
Tel: (612) 645 5029

RECOMMENDED
Hefe Weizen
(4.1%), spritzy and
refreshing in
Bavarian style
**Great Northern
Porter**
(5.4%), dry,
chocolatey,
and roasty

SUMMIT BREWING

One of America's "first wave" micros, and the classic ale-brewer in the Twin Cities (St. Paul and adjoining Minneapolis). Founder Mark Stutrud worked as a chemical dependency counselor before choosing craft-brewing as an "honest" living. Summit's small, copper brewhouse, manufactured in 1938, was purchased from the Hirschbrau brewery in Heimertingen, Bavaria. In 1997, it pushed the limits of its cap-acity when it produced 31,000 barrels (36,375hl) of beer. The company opened a new brewery (along West Seventh Street in Crosby Lake Business Park) in 1998 that will more than double Summit's capacity – eventually accommodating up to 300,000 barrels (352,000hl).

Summit offers four year-round beers: the gentle flagship Extra Pale Ale; a softly banana-fruity Hefe Weizen; an India Pale Ale,

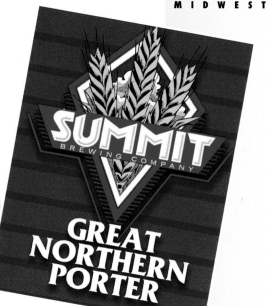

Summit's distribution is "steep and deep" – limited to the states around its home, yet very widespread within that region

which seems to have lost some hop character lately; and the distinctive Great Northern Porter, which captured a First Place award at the 1987 Great American Beer Festival. These are supported by three rotating seasonal beers: the smoothly-malty early spring Heimertingen Maibock, autumn Alt Bier, and medium-bodied Winter Ale.

The company's brews have a strong local following. You might even say, given Stutrud's previous career, that the Twin Cities are "hooked" on Summit's fresh, flavorful beers. With the brewery's new ability to expand, other regions may soon be reaching for a Summit.

Also worth trying

In Minnesota, Minnetonka's highly-regarded **Sherlock's Home** brewpub makes excellent (true) cask-conditioned ales. **James Page Brewing** of Minneapolis completed an expansion in 1997 to meet demand for its smooth Amber and pioneering Boundary Waters Wild Rice beer. To the east in Wisconsin, Milwaukee's **Sprecher Brewing** offers a year-round Black Bavarian lager and special seasonals such as an Imperial Stout. Janesville's **Gray Brewing** lets you wash down the state's trademark cheese curds with a deliciously hoppy

American Pale Ale and quaffable Oatmeal Stout.

Old regional **Leinenkugel Brewing** (now owned by Miller) rolls out accessible "specialties" like an Auburn Ale and Winter Lager (not to mention Big Butt Doppelbock) from both its Chippewa Falls headquarters and Milwaukee's ex-Val Blatz Brewery. **Stevens Point Brewery**, another long-standing regional, also has changed with the times by introducing brews like Point Bock, Winter Spice, and Maple Wheat.

Chicago's tiny **Golden Prairie Ale & Mead Co**. turns out a refreshing Honey Ginger Ale on occasion. Some Chicago bars serve suds from newcomer **Three Floyds Brewery**, located in Hammond, Indiana. Look for the hopped-to-drop Alpha King (the name refers to bittering value), made with four hop varieties. If Dorothy had been a beer drinker, she would have clicked her heels to get to the **Free State** brewpub in Lawrence, Kansas.

In the far southeast corner of the Midwest, the **Boston Beer Co.** bought Cincinnati's regional Hudepohl-Schoenling brewery in 1997 and now produces its Samuel Adams' line there. Owner Jim Koch's father worked as an apprentice brewmaster at the Hudy plant back in the 1940s.

Former Chicagoans include Full Sail Brewing founder Jerome Chicvara and porn star "Vixxxen." Ain't America great?

SOUTHWEST

Does a mention of the Southwest conjure up images of dusty cowboys quaffing cans of light American lager under an unforgiving sun? The region certainly does down its share of mainstream American beer: bland industrial brews such as Lone Star hold a place deep in the hearts of Texans, after all, and there's clearly a reason that Anheuser-Busch runs a megabrewery in Colorado's Fort Collins (beyond a desire to irritate Colorado-headquartered Coors). Overall, perhaps due in part to the region's climate, the progress of craft-brewing has been slower here than in other areas of North America.

But things are changing for the better. Today, beer lovers can buy brown ales in Boulder, hoist hand-pumped "cask ale" in Houston, and source several micros in Santa Fe. In Texas, Belgium's Pierre Celis creates classic brews in Austin that would be equally at home in Ostend. Even Coors – whose Golden, Colorado, facility is the largest single-site brewery in the world – crafts Imperial Stouts and

Raspberry Ales at its Sandlot brewpub in Denver's baseball stadium, Coors Field. There's no question that craft beer, like everything else in the Southwest, is heating up.

Keeping track of the region's dynamic beer scene can be more difficult than selling sand to a scorpion. Let *Southern Draft Brew News – Southwest Edition* (1290 Jean Place, Rio Rancho, New Mexico 87124) and *Southwest Brewing News* (1505 Lupine Lane, Austin, Texas 78741) do the reporting. The Association of Brewers (P.O. Box 1679, Boulder, Colorado 80306) tracks craft-brewing across the country and also organizes Denver's annual Great American Beer Festival.

EST. 1991

2431 Forbes Drive,
Austin,
Texas 78754
Tel: (512) 835 0884

RECOMMENDED

White
(4.8%), many
consider it the
classic witbier

Golden
(4.9%), refreshing,
clean, herbal-hoppy
Pilsner

Grand Cru
(8.7%), deliciously
finessed and
flavorful

CELIS BREWERY

★

Founded by veteran brewer Pierre Celis, who is famous for rescuing Belgium's nearly-lost "white beer" (witbier) style. After Belgian beer-giant Interbrew acquired his revivalist brewery in Hoegaarden, Belgium, Celis started afresh in America. Attracted to Austin in Texas by its soft limestone water (similar to Hoegaarden's), he began brewing new versions of his favorite beers.

The Celis Brewery, which features a classic copper brewhouse made in Belgium during the 1930s, stands several miles outside downtown Austin. In 1994, the Celis team raised capital by selling a majority interest to Miller Brewing. Jokes about "Miller White" continue to prove unjustified: if anything, Miller's influence (largely confined to marketing expertise) has helped Celis refocus its efforts.

Celis White is brewed from 50 percent barley malt and 50 percent raw Texas winter wheat. A traditional

RIGHT: *White beer from copper kettles! Celis imported both its flagship style and its brewhouse from Belgium.*

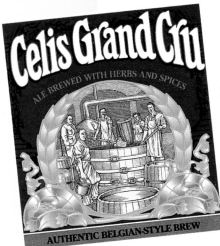

lactic fermentation leaves it tart and tangy with lots of wheaty flavor (the original Hoegaarden White seems "softer"). Curaçao and other spices give Grand Cru, a strong golden ale, lots of aromatic character and complexity.

Celis Golden is generously Saaz-hopped to create its zesty herbal aroma and flavor. Dubbel Ale, strong and dark in the "abbey" style, approaches the character of Hoegaarden's lush Forbidden Fruit. A candy-sweet Raspberry wheat beer and nutty Pale Ale (in the

Belgian-style) also are offered.

In 1998, Celis began limited production of a straw-colored, lightly hopped Pale Rider Ale in conjunction with film actor Clint Eastwood. Rumors suggest that Eastwood finalized the arrangement by saying, "Go ahead – make my beer."

RIGHT: *Pierre or Peter? The bi-national Celis remains a tireless advocate for the witbier style he reintroduced.*

EST. 1994
2201 Arapahoe,
Denver,
Colorado 80205
Tel: (303) 296 9460

RECOMMENDED
Arapahoe
Amber Ale
(5.9%), well-made
American amber
Hibernation Ale
(8.1%), warming
and hoppy,
worth seeking

GREAT DIVIDE BREWING

★

G reat Divide is a typical success story of the craft-brewing industry. When Brian Dunn developed his business plan in 1993, he couldn't imagine growth like 250 and 300 percent in the first two years – but that's exactly what happened. And Great Divide

RIGHT: *The textbook early-90s' start-up, from its cramped quarters to its utilitarian brewhouse and used equipment, Great Divide has seen unusual success.*

Great Divide takes its name from the watershed of the North American continent, also called the Continental Divide.

continues to grow at a healthy pace. It should produce about 6,000 barrels in 1998, with its beers sold in 12 states (mainly through the middle of the country).

Located in a building that housed a dairy business during the 1930s, Great Divide turns out six year-round beers and one thoroughly distinctive seasonal, Hibernation Ale. This mahogany "old ale" grabbed

a gold medal at a recent Great American Beer Festival. Of the year-round brews, the mouthfilling Arapahoe Amber is the brewery's flagship; fans in the know ask for 'Rapahoe. Other offerings include the clean and balanced Denver Pale Ale; Whitewater Wheat, an American-style wheat ale; Bee Sting Honey Ale, brewed with orange blossom honey; and Wild Raspberry Ale, made with both red and black raspberries. The popular Saint Brigid's Porter, (robust, slightly roasty) is named after the Irish saint who transformed her bath-water into beer for thirsty clerics. Sure beats turning water into wine!

195

EST. 1991
500 Linden Street,
Fort Collins,
Colorado 80524
Tel: (970) 221 0524

RECOMMENDED
Abbey
(6.5%), outstanding
spicy-fruity, dark malt
character
Trippel
(7.8%), fresh-tasting
hops balance
honeyed malt
Abbey Grand Cru
(8%), America's
answer to
Rochefort 8°

NEW BELGIUM

New Belgium's is a classic tale: homebrewer Jeff Lebesch and his wife decided to take their hobby commercial. The twist was their inspiration, the great ales of Belgium. Within their first year, demand forced the founders to move the brewery out of their home and into a purpose-built

RIGHT: *Who needs Doom or Quake when you can play with a brewhouse? Jeff Lebesch mans the controls.*

location. Production increased at an amazing rate, even for the craft-beer industry. To cope with the region's still-growing thirst, New Belgium moved into a $5-million new facility, complete with an advanced German-built Steinecker brewhouse, in 1995. Production of 80,000 barrels (98,000hl) in 1997 was spread over seven western states.

New Belgium's success rides on a fat tire – Fat Tire Amber Ale, to be precise. The shocking popularity of this simple-drinking amber has thrust it into the position of Colorado's top-selling ale. New Belgium's other beers are more distinctive. Look for a year-round Old Cherry Ale supplemented in late fall by a brown-ale-based Frambozen. Belgian aficionados will be keenly interested in the Abbey (dubbel) and Trippel, which the brewery says are fermented "with an authentic Belgian Trappist yeast." The Abbey Grand Cru, introduced to mark the company's 1,000th brew, now makes occasional reappearances whenever something needs celebrating.

New Belgium also is trying to draw attention to its brewing skills with a "special release program" showcasing a variety of traditional beer styles. Some of the beers featured in the program have been a gingery Belgian-style Saison, Porch Swing Ale (an abbey-style "single"), and Blue Paddle Pilsener.

EST. 1989
800 E. Lincoln,
Fort Collins,
Colorado 80524
Tel: (970) 498 9070

**RECOMMENDED
90 Shilling**
(5.5%), pleasantly
malty with
chocolate notes

ODELL BREWING

★

Until 1996, this family-run micro made only draft beers. Doug, Wynne, and Corkie Odell founded their namesake brewery at a relatively early time (at least for Colorado). Subsequent growth has been fueled by its malty, balanced 90 Shilling ale, which dominates taps across Fort Collins and the surrounding region. The brewery moved from its quaint original site, a historic grain elevator, to a new facility in 1994, which (after an expansion for bottling) has a 60,000-barrel (70,400hl) capacity.

Odell Brewing sold more than 17,300 barrels (20,300hl) in 1997, mostly in Colorado but also with limited

In Scotland a "90 Shilling" ale approaches heady, potent territory. Odell's interpretation is more modest.

distribution in five nearby states. In addition to the 90 Shilling – not the more potent brew its name suggests, but something of a cross between a Scottish "heavy" and an English pale ale – Odell features an unfiltered Easy Street Wheat (American-style), a "light" golden ale called Levity, and a Cutthroat Pale Ale and Porter (brewed with English Kent Goldings). There are also limited-production brews such as a robust Scotch Ale and an annual Christmas beer,

Holiday Shilling. A small run of Curmudgeon's Nip, a wonderfully complex barley-wine (9.5%, malt-driven), was offered in 1997 and may be brewed again.

Getting back to his creative roots, Doug Odell recently began brewing on a "small" 10-barrel system, rolling out limited runs of experimental ales available on draft.

"Nip" refers to small bottles (usually 7oz. or fewer) traditionally used to package the strongest of beers.

EST. 1979
2880 Wilderness
Place,
Boulder,
Colorado 80301
Tel: (303) 444 8448

RECOMMENDED
Boulder
Cliffhanger Ale
(4.2%), lots of fresh
hop flavor
Boulder Porter
(5.2%), pleasantly
smooth and sweetish
Boulder Stout
(5.8%), sweet,
complex, and
mouth-filling

ROCKIES BREWING *(Boulder Beers)*

T his sizable company has the distinction of being the oldest operating craft-brewery in America. Two homebrewers founded the original Boulder Brewing Company on a farm outside the city. The current purpose-built brewery and pub was raised in 1984. Six years later, however, management woes and quality-control problems sent Boulder into foreclosure. The brewery has been substantially revitalized under the guidance of buyer Gina Day, a former medical technologist.

With the help of experienced Pacific Northwest brewmaster David Zuckerman, Day put Boulder back on track: all recipes were reformulated, and the company name was changed (to Rockies) better to reflect its regional focus. Today, Rockies offers seven year-round Boulder Ales and five limited edition brews (such as spring's Cliffhanger, a lightly-fruity ale generously dry-hopped with Hallertau, and

The beers from Rockies are smooth and quaffable, though hopheads may wish they were "bolder."

summer's Single-track Copper Ale, brewed with flaked rye). The newest limited edition brew, Ultimate Weiss, is a hefeweizen with traditional Bavarian yeast. The clean-tasting Boulder Pale Ale and gutsy Amber Ale sell best throughout the year, although the Stout and Porter are more complex.

Rockies recently completed a 4,500-square-foot (418m²) expansion to increase its annual capacity to 60,000 barrels (70,400hl); about two-thirds of that was produced in 1998. With its 20-year anniversary approaching and distribution encompassing 22 states (from California to Florida), the brewery's future – despite the dynamic nature of the craft-brewing industry – should be anything but rocky.

Boulder Beers are crafted in the same town that hosts the offices of the American Homebrewers' Association.

206

EST. 1994

2522 Fairway
Park Drive,
Houston,
Texas 77092
Tel: (713) 686 9494

RECOMMENDED
Amber Ale

(5.5%), light citrusy
aroma, smooth
caramel flavors

SAINT ARNOLD BREWING

If you can name a porter after Saint Bridgid (see Great Divide), why not a brewery after Saint Arnold – the two would have made a perfect holy couple, after all. Recognized by the Catholic Church as the Patron Saint of Brewers, Saint Arnold spent his life in the 7th century warning peasants about the dangers of drinking water instead of beer. Inspired by the good Saint's fervor, as well as their own love for distinctive suds, Brock Wagner and Kevin Bartol (both former investment bankers) opened Houston's first microbrewery.

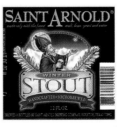

Wagner develops all Saint Arnold's recipes based on his home-brewing experience. His beers display an affinity for rich, malty, creamy flavors enhanced by a healthy dose of hops.

The flagship Amber Ale provides quaffable caramel maltiness (from Belgian Caravienne malt) to support aroma and flavor from Cascade and Liberty hops. It shines in cask-conditioned form – look for it at Houston's excellent GingerMan pub (5607 Morningside Drive). The brewery's other two year-round beers are Brown Ale, made with a combination of five malts and three American hops, and Kristall Weizen, a filtered wheat beer made with 40 percent malted wheat. A rotating array of five seasonal brews includes a Czech Saaz- and Tettnang-hopped Spring Bock; Summerfest, a Bohemian-style Pilsner; and a creamy, full-bodied Winter Stout alongside the limited-run Christmas Ale. Thank you, Saint Arnold, for answering Houston's beery prayers.

EST. 1993
1265 Boston Avenue,
Longmont,
Colorado 80501
Tel: (303) 293 2253

RECOMMENDED
Tabernash Munich
(4.9%), a smooth and
nutty dunkel
Tabernash Weiss
(5.7%), one of
America's best
Bavarian-style
wheats
Tabernash Maibock
(7.2%), well bal-
anced,
deceptively smooth

TABERNASH/LEFT HAND
BREWING

★

N amed after an old stagecoach
station in the Colorado mountains, Tabernash has a distinguished
pedigree: founding brewmaster
Eric Warner (who has left the
company) earned a diploma from
Germany's famous Weihenstephan
brewing school, while co-founder
Jeff Mendel previously directed

RIGHT: *Brewer Bill Hasse checks a complex
piece of equipment called a "trash can."*

America's micro-watching Institute for Brewing Studies. Warner literally "wrote the book" on weizens (his *German Wheat Beer* is an acknowledged industry reference). Tabernash's crisp, tangy, unfiltered Weiss, considered by many to be the country's best Bavarian example, still illustrates his skill.

Excepting the Weiss, all Tabernash's year-round beers are lagers. The founders chose this path to distinguish the company from Colorado's several ale breweries. Respectable lagering time makes both the malty Munich Dark Lager and Saaz-scented Golden Pilsner smooth and subtle. Tabernash Amber is an interpretation of a "steam beer" (once a style common throughout the West). Seasonals such as the fall's Oktoberfest and springtime's Maibock are appropriately richer in character. Tabernash beers can be found primarily in Colorado, but also in selected markets in six other states.

Tabernash operated out of Denver's historic Denargo Market until 1998, when – in an attempt to overcome an industry slowdown – it joined forces with Left Hand Brewing of Longmont, Colorado, and relocated its operation to Left Hand's expanded brewery. Left Hand, perhaps best known for its spiced Juju Ginger Ale, offers several traditional English-inspired brews: the citrusy-hoppy, smooth Jackman's Pale Ale (5.1%) is best.

Tabernash was one of the earliest American micros to position a Bavarian-style wheat beer as its flagship brew

213

EST. 1988
1634 18th Street,
Denver,
Colorado 80202
Tel: (303) 297 2700

RECOMMENDED
St. Charles ESB
(4.7%), smoothly
malty with
balancing hop
Sagebrush Stout
(5%), hearty,
extra-smooth (from
oatmeal)
India Pale Ale
(5.5%), especially
refreshing on
hand-pump

WYNKOOP BREWING

T his pioneering Colorado brew-pub, the oldest in the state, is named after Denver's first sheriff Edward Wynkoop (1836–1891) – well, actually it's really named after near by Wynkoop Street, which is named after the first sheriff. (And if you think that's confusing, try pronouncing the name!). Located a few blocks from Coors Field in Denver's renovated, trendy "Lo(wer) Do(wntown)" area, Wynkoop was founded by former geologist John Hickenlooper, who subsequently helped open several other brewpubs and breweries across Colorado and several other states. If there is a

"godfather" of American brewpubs, Hickenlooper is he.

The flagship Wynkoop brew is RailYard Ale, billed as a union of English Pale Ale and German Oktoberfest lager. Other year-round beers include the IPA, ESB, and Stout. These are supplemented by a wide rotating range that has

RIGHT: *"Tray chic?" A smiling server offers up samples of Wynkoop's line, including RailYard Ale.*

included a chocolatey Scottish Ale and peach-flavored BackYard Ale. RailYard and occasional other beers are brewed separately for bottling by nearby Broadway Brewing. Broadway was established jointly by Wynkoop and Aspen's Flying Dog Brewery as a commercial brewing and bottling facility.

Wynkoop claims bragging rights for being the largest brewpub in America (based on annual volume, over 4,000 barrels/4,700hl) and the second largest in the world, behind Prague's U Fleku – with which it is locked in perpetual struggle. Such size gives it the means to support events like the Beer Drinker Of The Year contest (interested contenders can submit their "beer resumés") and Denver's infamous "running of the pigs" (down LoDo streets).

RIGHT: *The installation of a trolley system in Denver let Wynkoop celebrate with a play on its flagship RailYard.*

SOLSTICE WINTER ALE

WYNKOOP BREWING COMPANY

LIGHT RAIL ALE

(650 ml)
1 Pint 6 Fluid oz.

WYNKOOP BREWING COMPANY

On
Average
Analysis
each 12 oz. bottle
contains: 142 calories
4.7 grams carbohydrates
1.0 grams protein
0.0 grams fat

Brewed and bottled by Broadway Brewing LLC, Denver, Colorado
exclusively for Wynkoop Brewing Company, Denver, Colorado.

EST. 1994
17201 San Pedro
Ave,
San Antonio,
Texas 78232
Tel: (210) 496 6669

RECOMMENDED
Yellow Rose
Pale Ale
(5.1%), the brewery's
flagship ale
Honcho Grande
Brown Ale
(5.1%), smooth,
hearty, and
slightly nutty
Wildcatter's
Refined Stout
(5.6%), dark and
thick like Texas crude

218

YELLOW ROSE BREWING

This enthusiastic micro was founded by a former oral surgeon who now can claim to be "treating" Texan palates with his robust English-style ales. Yellow Rose operates in a converted ice-house in the city that Lone Star beer made famous. The homemade brewhouse, a 10-barrel system with an annual capacity of 2,300 barrels (2,700hl), produces seven year-round ales available on draft

throughout San Antonio and in other Texas metro areas (as well as selected markets in a few nearby states). In addition to draft, Yellow Rose's beers can be found packaged in individual longneck pint bottles with wrap-around labels that offer lessons in regional history. 1998

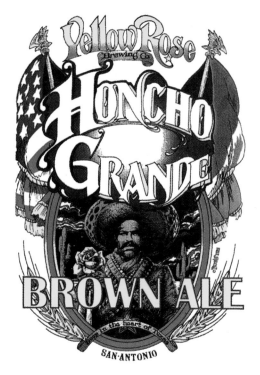

"Slightly nutty" describes both the beer and, depending on your politics, Mexico's famous bandit/ revolutionary on the label.

saw Yellow Rose pushing the 2,000 barrel (2,350hl) mark.

In addition to its signature Pale Ale and Honcho Grande ("big guy") brown, inspired by legendary Mexican revolutionary Pancho Villa, Yellow Rose offers a moderately dry Vigilante Porter and the semi-sweet Wildcatter's Refined Stout. The range also includes an American-style honey wheat beer dubbed Bubba Dog and the hoppy Cactus Queen India Pale Ale. As its beer names suggest, the folks at Yellow Rose make every effort to enjoy themselves. Microbrewing is a tough job, reports the company's newsletter, but "it beats canning fish!" No argument there.

RIGHT: *The Yellow Rose crew pose with some "Bubba" dogs in front of their fully modernized delivery fleet.*

Also worth trying

Texas maintains a tradition of American "bocks" – caramel-accented versions of mainstream lagers – best represented by Shiner Bock from old regional **Spoetzl Brewing**. Spoetzl's corporate parent, the **Gambrinus Company** (which imports Corona and Moosehead beers), has introduced a light summer seasonal and malty Winter Ale under the **Shiner** banner. In 1998, Gambrinus – which already owned Oregon's BridgePort Brewing – purchased Pete's Brewing Company, the country's second-largest contract brewer. Back in Texas itself, the state's many brew-

pubs (Austin's **Bitter End** and **Routh Street** in Dallas, for example) offer more interesting beers. Austin's multi-tapped GingerMan beer bar (304 West 4th Street) usually serves the fruity Balcones Red Granite Ale from nearby **Hill Country Brewing**.

Arizona, already awash in brewpubs, is developing a taste for German-style beers from fledgling micro **McFarlane Brewing** in Phoenix. Tempe's **Four Peaks** offers draft ales that include a peat-smoked Scottish Amber and mellow Oatmeal Stout. Neighboring New Mexico also has its share of micros and brewpubs. Of the former, Santa Fe's

Russell Brewing crafts several specialties in 22-ounce bottles, while long-established **Santa Fe Brewing** produces a big-bodied Fiesta IPA and seasonals such as Dark Wheat (a German-style dunkelweizen).

In Utah, restrictive "3.2" (alcohol content by weight) laws have hampered the specialty beer movement. Nevertheless, several brewpubs – particularly Salt Lake City's **Desert Edge**, **Wasatch**, and **Squatters** – make several distinctive beers in traditional styles.

Colorado's 60-plus small brewers and brewpubs compose the region's most developed beer market.

HC Berger Brewing, an early Ft. Collins micro, bottles an award-winning Maibock as part of its "brewmaster's special choice" line. Boulder's **Avery Brewing** offers a mouthfilling Out Of Bounds Stout and smooth Ellie's Brown Ale (whose original name raised the wrath of womans' magazine *Elle*). Some of the state's popular brewpubs include Aspen's **Flying Dog**, Boulder's **Walnut**, Denver's **Chophouse**, Fort Collins' **Coopersmiths**, the multiple-location **Breckenridge Breweries & Pubs**, and Colorado Springs' **Phantom Canyon** (famous for a lightly-smoky Peated Porter).

CALIFORNIA

California is famous for movements both seismic and cultural. From San Francisco's Beat poets to San Diego's surf-speak to L.A.'s latest batch of snappy sitcom phrases, plenty of social trends originate in the Golden State. So it is with craft-brewing. California not only hosts Anchor Brewing, the resuscitated regional that pioneered modern specialty beers, but also gave birth to America's first "official" micro-brewery, New Albion, in the late 1970s.

Although New Albion proved ahead of its time, its philosophy has been carried forward by a wave of California craft-breweries that includes everyone from sizeable Sierra Nevada to bite-size Bison Brewing. Specialty beer has even spread west to Hawaii (where islanders say "aloha!" to a Gordon Biersch brewpub and a few local start-ups). Lots of thirsty California consumers support the movement's growth. The San Francisco Bay Area alone contains more than twice Washington state's total population (which may explain why Seattle's Pyramid breweries opened a large plant in Berkeley).

Like many successful California brewers, the excellent *Celebrator Beer News* (P.O. Box 375, Hayward, California 94545) covers the state while also addressing the overall country.

EST. 1896
1705 Mariposa Street
San Francisco,
California 94107
Tel: (415) 863 8350

RECOMMENDED
Steam Beer
(5%), malty-nutty,
dry, and hoppy
Liberty Ale
(6%), supremely
hoppy, aromatic
pale ale
Old Foghorn
(8.7%), beautifully
balanced, richly
complex
barley wine

ANCHOR BREWING

A San Francisco legend now so famous for its Steam Beer that fans frequently refer to the whole brewery as "Anchor Steam." In the 1960s, however, Anchor was sinking fast before Fritz Maytag (heir to the washing-machine family), a recent graduate from nearby Stanford University, learned of its imminent demise while enjoying a glass of Steam. His initial offer to help save the company turned into an outright purchase in 1965.

Over the next decade, Maytag tirelessly worked to revive both the brewery and its beers. Ultimately, Anchor products became so popular that Maytag could afford to move out of the company's old, rundown facility. He built a new showplace brewery – with a hand-made copper brewhouse – in a restored coffee factory. To Maytag's eternal credit, he shared his brewery experiences with the new generation of small brewers in the late 1970s and helped launch

Demand for its internationally popular beers means Anchor's cup truly runneth over.

North America's craft-beer renaissance.

Anchor's flagship Steam Beer (fermented with lager yeast at "ale" temperatures) defines the eponymous, indigenous American beer style. It is joined year-round by Liberty Ale, Old Foghorn, a rich stout-like Porter, and extremely clean-tasting Wheat Beer (American style). The golden Liberty shows an incredible Cascade-hop aroma and flavor. Foghorn, whose name resonates with San Francisco character, offers a seamless blend of rich malt, estery fruit, and herbal hop; in 1998, the brewery began experimenting with an "Anchor Small Beer" made from Foghorn's second runnings. Many fans "lay down" Old Foghorn bottles to mature. The same goes for Anchor's vintage-dated Christmas Ale. Technically called "Our Special Ale," it is brewed to a different recipe each year (the past several have yielded spiced brown ales).

With the possible exception of the Wheat, all of Maytag's beers have helped inspire countless new microbrewers. Anchor's pioneering significance cannot be overstated.

LEFT: *Fritz Maytag in a "family portrait" with the Anchor line.*
RIGHT: *Anchor's copper brewhouse (top) feeds rich wort into the special open, shallow fermenters used for Steam Beer.*

EST. 1987

14081 Highway 128,
Boonville,
California 95415
Tel: (707) 895 2337

RECOMMENDED
Deep Enders Dark
Porter
(5%), smooth and
medium-bodied
Barney Flats
Oatmeal Stout
(5.3%), rich, sweetish,
deeply roasted
Hop Ottin' IPA
(7%), fruity,
bursting with
citrus hop notes

ANDERSON VALLEY
BREWING

An iconoclastic micro in Mendocino County's rural Anderson Valley, growing at a regular rate. In 1996, the company supplemented its original 10-barrel brewhouse – serving the on-premises Buckhorn Saloon – with a temporary 30-barrel sys-

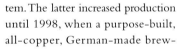

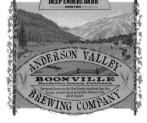

tem. The latter increased production until 1998, when a purpose-built, all-copper, German-made brewhouse (capable of 100-barrel/117hl batches) came on-line. As a result, Anderson Valley plans to expand distribution beyond its stronghold in California. The Saloon's

10-barrel system will be retained for "pilot" and special brews.

Anderson Valley offers several year-round ales, all named in the region's "Boontling" dialect (created by the isolated valley's residents in the

RIGHT: *The beers' names are strange – and the local dialect even more odd – but Anderson Valley's ales are certainly well worth seeking out.*

late 19th century). Hop Ottin' IPA, which translates to "hard working hops," is stuffed to the seams (90 bitterness units!) with the intense citrus character of Columbus hops. The complex (dry hopped?) Boont Amber, extremely well-balanced Porter,

LEFT: *A brewer with a backbone! Former chiropractor Ken Allen founded Anderson Valley and today keeps the brewery (and its staff?) snapped into shape.*

232

and slightly oily (in a good way) Oatmeal Stout also draw praise.

Anderson Valley additionally offers a clean, refreshing High Rollers Wheat, soft and bitter Poleeko Gold Pale Ale, and malty-sweetish Belks ESB. Occasional special brews include a rare Barley Wine and the annual Winter Solstice, which is seasoned with "secret" spices.

BEAR REPUBLIC BREWING

EST. 1996
345 Healdsburg
Avenue,
Healdsburg,
California 95448
Tel: (707) 433 2337

RECOMMENDED
Nitro Stout
(4.2%), soft, creamy,
mocha flavors
Red Rocket Ale
(6.8%), assertively
hopped chocolatey
flavors

Founded by a homebrewer whose obsession for mountain biking only was equaled by his thirst for ale. The brewery name derives from the California state flag (and reflects an 1846 insurrection by U.S. patriots, who briefly took control of the region, which was then a protectorate of Mexico).

The father/son team of Richard R. Norgrove and Richard G. (the younger) have created a brewpub and microbrewery producing big,

uncompromising ales in the heart of California's Sonoma County wine country. Amid the "late handlebar" décor of racing jerseys and bike memorabilia, the Bear Republic pub usually hosts winery staff from the surrounding area relaxing with the "fruit of the grain" after a hard day at work.

RIGHT: *After a long day, personnel from surrounding Sonoma Valley's wineries like nothing better than coming here to "grin and Bear it."*

of grape-related work. To address growing demand, a major brewery expansion was completed in 1998. The 16-barrel brewhouse offers a broad range of Bear Republic beers. These include the flagship Red Rocket (described as a "bastard-ized Scottish style"), a nitrogenated creamy stout, an American-style wheat ale, a soft pale ale, a stronger-than-average ESB, and an herbal-tinged IPA. Specialties include Racer 5 (5.9%, unfiltered, featuring Columbus hops; dry-hopped with Cascades) – a beer inspired by the Japanese cartoon *Speed Racer* – and several rotating seasonals.

Although the original 1846 Bear Republic was short-lived (25 days), observers are bullish on the success of this modern beer-based namesake. A trip to northern California without sampling the company's fine brews would be simply un*bear*able!

LEFT: *"Och, laddie" meets "hey, dude" – Red Rocket is described as a bastardized Scottish ale, California style.*
RIGHT: *More functional than aesthetic, Bear Republic's stainless steel brewhouse.*

EST. 1988

2 Harrison Street,
San Francisco,
California 94105
Tel: (415) 243 8246

RECOMMENDED
Weizen

(4.5%), soft
and aromatic in
Bavarian style

GORDON BIERSCH

A pioneering brewpub chain founded by restauranteur Dean Biersch and brewer Dan Gordon, who learned his craft at Germany's famous Weihenstephan brewing school. Locations across California – San Jose (33 E. San Fernando Street), Pasadena (41 Hugus Alley), City of Orange (1623 W. Katella) and flagship San Francisco – now supplement their original Palo Alto site (640 Emerson). The company also is expanding outside the state, with brewpubs in Honolulu, Hawaii (1 Aloha Tower Drive, #1123) and other major cities (including Seattle). All display a kind of upscale-yet-casual "California style."

Attracted by the chain's success, a large Las Vegas-based entertainment group purchased a controlling interest in Gordon Biersch at the end of 1995 (the chain's administrative headquarters now are found in the Nevada city). Gordon Biersch used this infusion of capital to construct a full-production brewery (with a 50,000-barrel/58,700hl annual capacity) in San Jose (357 E. Taylor).

Gordon Biersch specializes in classic German lagers. One notable exception is the unfiltered Weizen, introduced at the Hawaii location but now available seasonally throughout the chain. The company's hoppy Pilsner, balanced Märzen, and caramel-accented Dunkles are available year-round at the brewpubs. Additionally, the brewpubs offer specialties such as spring's Maibock and fall's Dunkelweizen. Since October 1996, the Pilsner and Märzen also have been available in bottles. A third bottled beer, Blond Bock, was introduced as a seasonal but looks likely to become year-round: this full-bodied, rich strong lager deservedly is one of Gordon Biersch' most popular brews.

A sight for thirsty commuters? Gordon Biersch's San Francisco location stands almost under the well-travelled Bay Bridge.

EST. 1987
856 10th Street,
Arcata,
California 95221
Tel: (707) 826 1734

RECOMMENDED
Red Nectar
(5.3%),
a fruity-hoppy
"American
amber ale"

HUMBOLDT BREWING

S ituated in northern California's Humboldt County, approximately halfway between San Diego and Seattle, the company has expanded substantially since Mario Celotto, a former Oakland Raiders football player (and Super Bowl winner), first founded it as a brewpub: production jumped from 1,200 barrels (1,400hl) in 1992 to more than 18,000 (21,100hl) in 1998! Distribution encompasses all of California and pockets of Oregon, Nevada, and Hawaii. What's driving this

RIGHT: *Humboldt's prosaic brewhouse stands in sharp contrast to the lush woodlands around Arcata.*

240

sweet growth? Humboldt's flagship Red Nectar, which balances a notable hop profile (Chinook, Willamette, Mt. Hood, Cascade) with solid malty, fruity depth.

It is available year-round along with Gold Nectar, a hoppy American pale ale. Humboldt's Hemp Ale is a tribute to the other major crop, besides Redwoods, that many believe grows in the region's forests. Hemp seeds lend an herbal and soft, slightly nutty flavor to this toasty reddish beer, which is brewed with Chinooks, Willamettes, and Tettnangs. While popularity of hemp suds may turn out to be fleeting, Humboldt's version surely is one of the more interesting attempts. Visitors to the company's

Arcata pub can look for specialties such as an Oatmeal Stout and Hefeweizen (both now also in bottles), as well as a seasonal Cheshire Cat barley wine. Overall, Humboldt's Celotto looks set to replicate his football success in the (on the?) brewing field.

RIGHT: *"Bah, Humboldt!" is a sentiment seldom expressed inside the brewery's comfortable pub, where beer lovers gather to try the latest specialties.*

617 4th Street,
Eureka,
California 95501
Tel: (707) 445 4480

RECOMMENDED
Downtown
Brown
(4.8%), soft malty
nut-brown ale
Alleycat
Amber Ale
(4.9%), roasty hints,
caramel malts,
firmly hopped

LOST COAST
BREWERY & CAFE

L ost Coast is found in Eureka! The brewery stands in a renovated, 100-year old Victorian building located in the historic old town section of the city. Lost Coast was the first micro in America founded by women: Wendy Pound (a family counselor) and Barbara Groom (a pharmacist)

opened the company after years of meticulous hands-on research – extensive homebrewing and several trips to England to experience traditional British-style ales and

RIGHT: *"Tanks for the mammaries"? Female brewer Groom works magic in Lost Coast's expanded brewhouse.*

pubs. "Brewster" Groom continues to oversee the brewing and bottling of the Lost Coast products, which enjoy wide distribution throughout northern California and beyond.

The brewery is noted for richly flavorful beers and delightfully whimsical labels. Be sure to seek out the wonderful, refreshing Belgian-style witbier called Great White; the label features an aggravated shark holding a beer in one fin and a surfboard (with a bite mark in it) in the other. Feeling behind the 8-ball? Get rolling with Lost Coast's Eight-ball Stout (a hearty concoction of roasted malts, oatmeal for a softer texture and assertive hop bittering). Is there something magical about Eight-ball's satisfying character? "All signs point to yes."

The north coast lumber town of Eureka may have its contingent of out-of-work loggers, but the ales are fully employed – thanks to Lost Coast Brewery.

RIGHT: *Picasso would be proud – not only of the disjointed artwork on Downtown Brown's label, but also of the character of the beer itself.*

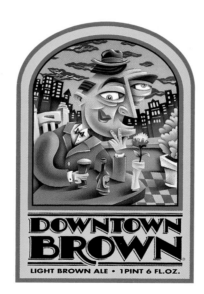

247

EST. 1989
P.O. Box 767,
Blue Lake,
California 95525
Tel: (707) 668 4151

RECOMMENDED
Jamaica Red Ale
(4.8%),
aggressively
hoppy and fruity
Jamaica Sunset
(5.8%),
citrusy-hoppy
IPA with complex
character

MAD RIVER BREWING

★

The company is named after a river (full of Steelhead salmon) in Humboldt County. Brewery founder Robert Smith previously worked at Humboldt Brewing, Sierra Nevada, and Eureka's Lost Coast Brewery. At Mad River, he brews with Sierra Nevada's original 17-barrel system and open square fermenters. Distribution encompasses the west and a few mid-Atlantic markets.

Mad River's beers are naturally carbonated and minimally filtered – a process that works best for the pleasantly

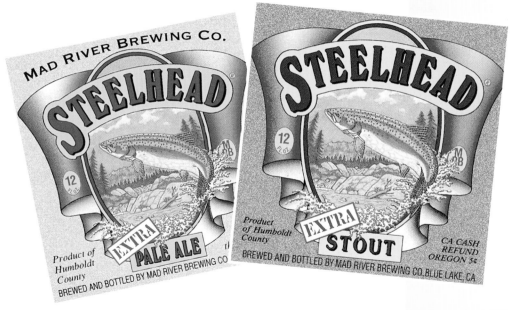

249

CELEBRATING
1995
HARVEST

12
FL. OZ.

JOHN BARLEYCORN
BARLEYWINE STYLE ALE
BREWED AND BOTTLED BY MAD RIVER BREWING CO., BLUE LAKE, CA

"rough hewn" Jamaica Red, with its richly fruity, hoppy, and darkly-malty character (similarities with Humboldt's Red Nectar are under-standable and, perhaps, undeniable). While minimal filtration also favors the creamy Steelhead Extra Stout, brewery flagship Steelhead Extra Pale Ale

might benefit from a clearer perspective. The deep-golden Jamaica Sunset, brewed from only extra pale malt, is hopped with Cluster, Cascade, Chinook, and Willamette in six separate additions; the result is a balanced, complex IPA with a long, long finish. Mad River also offers a winter seasonal, John Barleycorn barley wine, brewed to a slightly different recipe each year. The 1998 bottling (made with fresh ginger root and local wildflower honey) reached more than nine percent alcohol by volume! Anyone able to work through a few bottles truly can be said to have a "steel head."

The potency of Mad River's barleywine could make the rock group Traffic ("John Barleycorn Must Die") change its tune.

251

EST. 1983

13351 Hwy. 101 S.
Hopland,
California 95449
Tel: (707) 744 1015

RECOMMENDED
Black Hawk Stout
(5.8%), roasty,
fruity, and extremely
quaffable
Red Tail Ale
(6.4%), toasty-malt
balances fruity
character
Eye of the Hawk
(7.7%), potent,
limited-release
amber ale

MENDOCINO BREWING

This pioneering brewery in California's wine country is located in a town that (as its name suggests) once cultivated hops. Mendocino offers a taste of micro-brewing history: two of the founders worked for micro-pioneer New Albion. In fact, Mendocino began with New Albion's used equipment and fruity yeast (still in use today).

Like many early start-ups, the original brewpub quickly expanded to meet demand. Mendocino held a direct public stock offering in 1995 (raising approximately \$3.6 million) to fund construction of a second, larger brewery. This new facility is based 12 miles (19km) north in Ukiah, California. In 1997, Mendocino entered an "alliance" with United Breweries of America (owned by Indian entrepreneur

RIGHT: *Cleaning a primary fermenter in Mendocino's brewhouse – perhaps one that holds the elusive, high-flying "Eye."*

Vejay Malya, the mastermind behind India's Kingfisher Lager). Malya has started brewing Red Tail for east coast distribution at United Breweries' 10 Springs Brewery in Sarasota Springs, New York.

Mendocino flies high on bird-named beers: Red Tail Ale, Blue Heron Pale Ale, and Black Hawk Stout. The flagship Red Tail is dry and quaffable; Black Hawk offers a similar drinkability, along with roasty, sweet-coffee notes. Blue Heron is styled as fruity-bitter IPA. The Hopland brewpub also pours draft specialties such as the year-round Peregrine Pale Ale and winter's Yuletide Porter. Eye of the Hawk ("The Eye") is brewed and

bottled in limited quantities three times each year. Despite its name, this supremely balanced strong ale is certainly no featherweight.

Mendocino acquired Carmel Brewing of Salinas in 1998 and now produces Carmel beers (including an American-style hefeweizen) out of its Ukiah facility.

LEFT AND RIGHT: *From kettle to glass. Mendocino's Don Barkley hoists a manly mug of Black Hawk stout.*

EST. 1987

455 N. Main Street,
Fort Bragg,
California 95437
Tel: (707) 964 2739

RECOMMENDED
Old No. 38 Stout
(5.2%), deliciously
smooth and roasty
Red Seal Ale
(5.4%), cleanly
fruity and extremely
hoppy
Old Rasputin
Russian
Imperial Stout
(9.2%), excellent
interpretation of style

NORTH COAST BREWING

★

This brewery and pub is found in northern California's coastal Fort Bragg. Despite the location, a former mortuary, interest in North Coast's beers is extremely "lively" – so much so that during 1995 the company built a new, bigger brewhouse with a bottling line to supplement its original pub brewery. Red Seal Ale and the two stouts are available throughout the year, along with a Blue Star Wheat (American style) and Scrimshaw Beer (a Pilsner). Seasonals include an Oktoberfest and smooth Traditional Bock (both ales), as well

RIGHT: *All kegged up and ready to roll! North Coast's 1998 production approached 10,000 barrels (11,730hl) on the basis of acclaimed brews like Old Rasputin.*

as the Düsseldorf-inspired Alt Nouveau. North Coast crafts a second range of beers under its Acme label (revived from an old California regional brewery).

North Coast's signature beer, the toasty-malty Red Seal, bursts with bright, citric American hop character. Old No. 38, named for a retired steam-engine on Fort Bragg's railroad, is mellow but full of roasty-malt flavor. Old Rasputin offers the requisite intense notes of complex

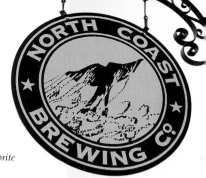

ripe fruit, warming alcohol, and "burnt" flavors – it occasionally is served with nitrogen for a deep, smooth, creamy character. North Coast's Belgian-inspired PranQster, a strong golden ale with plenty of fruity complexity, is best described as "Duvelishly delightful!"

With widespread distribution from California to North Carolina, there's no question that North Coast is giving its hometown something to Bragg about.

BELOW: *North Coast's revived Acme line is rumored to be a favorite brew of Wiley E. Coyote.*

259

EST. 1997
13250 River Road,
Guerneville,
California 95446
Tel: (707) 887 2294

RECOMMENDED
Pale Ale
(5.3%), subtle "best"
coast-style ale
Amber Ale
(5.6%), rich amber
color, spicy hop
character
Porter
(5.6%), soft mocha
malt flavors,
balanced

RUSSIAN RIVER BREWING

★

T alk about beer on a champagne budget! This showplace brewery is owned by the Korbel Winery and Champagne Cellars, which has been making wine along the banks of California's Russian River since 1882. (Logos and label artwork for the brewery show images of the Russian River traveling through the region's redwoods). Well known across the U.S. for its top-selling sparkling wines and brandy, Korbel is seeing its new brewing operation enjoy great success as well. Russian River's Porter, for example, has won

RIGHT: *It's always a good "vintage" in Russian River's brewhouse, regardless of the Sonoma grape harvest's quality.*

back-to-back medals in 1997 and 1998 at the national Great American Beer Festival. Korbel's vast "champagne budget" allowed for a state-of-the-art copper-clad brewhouse with four fermenters and four bright beer tanks. Currently, the 17-barrel brewhouse can craft up to 1,200 barrels (1,400hl) per year. Winemaker/enologist Randy Meyer is the brewery manager and Vinnie Cilurzo is brewmaster. Vinnie's background includes owner/brewer responsibilities at the original Blind Pig microbrewery in Temecula, California.

Four distinctive beers are served at the winery/brewery's restaurant and are distributed in bottles and on draft throughout northern California. These include a clean, quaffable Golden Wheat Ale and soft, fresh-tasting Pale Ale in the west coast style. Russian River's deeply-colored, spicily-hopped Amber Ale features five malts and four hops (Chinook, Centennial, Cascade, Kent Goldings), while the smooth, richly satisfying Porter gets its mellow complexity from eight different malts. The company also offers a big-bodied, draft-only IPA. Wine country visitors who thirst for distinctive ale should be rushin' to try these well-made brews.

RIGHT: *Look, Ma, no corks! Randy Meyer (left) and Vinnie Cilurzo.*

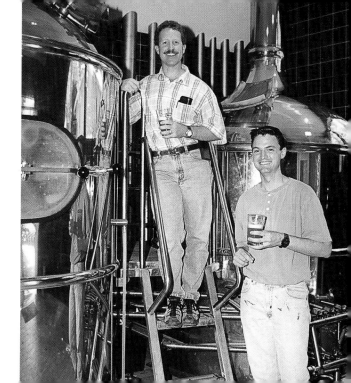

EST. 1981
1075 E. 20th Street,
Chico,
California 95928
Tel: (916) 893 3520

RECOMMENDED
Pale Ale
(5.5%), a delightfully
hoppy and
complex classic
Porter
(5.8%), fruity,
hoppy, coffeeish, and
drinkable
Bigfoot Ale
(10.1%), hugely
malty-rich and
exceedingly hoppy

SIERRA NEVADA BREWING

If Anchor Brewing is the "father" of American micros, Sierra Nevada is the big brother that everyone worships. Founder Ken Grossman, who opened the brewery as a young homebrewer, must be amazed at how his hoppy, complex ales have captivated the country: the brewery expected to sell some 350,000 barrels (410,700hl) in 1998. Sierra's purpose-built, showplace brewery opened in 1989

RIGHT: *All hail gallons of Pale Ale! A far cry from Sierra Nevada's "micro" start.*

Sierra's new
brewhouse has
dramatically
increased its
capacity, to
the delight of
beer lovers
everywhere.

(replacing the converted dairy-equipment original). A recent expansion should help cope with seemingly-insatiable demand. The attached pub offers draft specialties in addition to the regular range.

Sierra's medal-after-medal-winning Pale Ale, deeply complex and refreshing, defines the American "west coast" style. The Porter remains one of the country's, if not the world's, best. Sierra's eminently satisfying Stout, also powerfully hopped, is big, dry, and extremely roasty. In late fall Sierra releases its always eagerly-awaited Celebration Ale, a deep-copper brew that can be startlingly hoppy. Late winter brings Bigfoot, an almost overpoweringly malty and hoppy barley wine named for a mythical beast that haunts the Sierras. This beer can benefit from at least a year's maturation, although the brewers say they like it as fresh as possible. Other seasonals include a highly-hopped and dangerously drinkable Spring Bock, and a quenching Summerfest lager (hopped with classic German varieties).

Despite explosive growth, Sierra has not compromised the distinctive character of its outstanding beers. Their quality standard remains as sturdy as the mountain range after which the company is named.

RIGHT: *You can always find a few special brews on tap at Sierra Nevada's comfortable on-site pub.*

EST. 1997
14335 Sonoma
Highway 12,
Glen Ellen,
California 95442
Tel: (707) 935 4500

RECOMMENDED
Golden Pilsner
(4.5%), bright,
clean, crisply
hopped

SONOMA MOUNTAIN BREWING

★

When the winemaking Benzinger family had to rip out Merlot vines on their estate, they replanted with hops. Today, there are seven different hop varieties on location near Glen Ellen in Jack London's beloved "Valley of the Moon" – all of which go into beers produced on-site by the Benzinger's new Sonoma Mountain Brewery.

Bob Benzinger's decade-old infatuation with craft-brewing caught hold with his siblings, and

RIGHT: *You can't just crush them to make beer – Mike Benzinger (right) in Sonoma Mountain's hop fields.*

before long Mike Benzinger and brother-in-law Tim Wallace were studying everything they could about the beer business. Their Sonoma Mountain Brewery is the result. Its beautiful copper-and-tile, 50-barrel brewhouse was imported from a defunct brewery in Germany's Black Forest. Annual capacity stands at 10,000 barrels (11,730 hl).

Sonoma Mountain Golden Pilsner is a knockout – truly worthy of the much misused term "Pilsner." While not redolent of Saaz hops like the classic Czech brews, the aroma of the Golden Pilsner is a refreshing blast of hop fragrances blended from Tettnang, Saaz, Willamette, Liberty, Cascade, and Mt. Hood. The rich malty flavor gives way to a powerful uncompromising bittering that finishes dry and begs for a second taste.

The Sonoma Mountain Amber Lager, a beautiful mahogany color, shows a distinct malty character with balancing spicy hops (enough to break it out of the sweeter Märzen style). Both it and the Pils experience respectable lagering time—four to six weeks—a period that must seem extremely brief for a company used to long-lived Cabernets, Zinfandels, and Merlots.

RIGHT: *Inside Benzinger's Sonoma Mountain brewery, tanks and pipes take the place of rows of oak barrels.*

EST. 1984
821 L Street,
Modesto,
California 95354
Tel: (209) 524 2337

RECOMMENDED
Whistle Stop
Pale Ale
(4.6%), crisp,
refreshing and
thoroughly hoppy
Amber Alt
(5.8%), clean-tasting
with fresh hop
character
Red Sky Ale
(6%), smooth, nutty
malt and strong hops

ST. STAN'S BREWING

St. Stan's is the largest altbier producer in America. Around ten years after travel in Germany inspired founder Garith Helm and his wife to take up home brewing, they built a small brewery next to their house to produce a commercial version of their favorite alt style. In 1990, rising demand prompted the opening of St. Stan's current brewery (which incorporates a pub and restaurant). The company distributes widely in California, as well as several farther flung markets.

RIGHT: *There's nothing Modest(o) about these two out-Standing California ales.*

PALE ALE

S⸱T STAN'S

WHISTLE STOP ALE

A California Microbrewed Pale Ale

12 FLUID OUNCES

S⸱T STAN'S

RED SKY ALE

A California Microbrewed Red Ale

12 FLUID OUNCES

St. Stan's (known for altbier) occasionally offers a wheat, while Oregon's Widmer (known for wheat) sometimes brews an alt. Coincidence?

Altbier remains a focus (leading some to call it California's "altimate" beer experience): alongside the flagship Amber, St. Stan's offers a chocolatey Dark Alt and wintertime "Fest" version. The brewery also has expanded its styles in recent years with Red Sky Ale and Whistle Stop Pale Ale, two beers in California's hoppy micro tradition (although they are brewed from traditional English hops in addition to aggressive American ones). Visitors to the Modesto brewery are likely to find additional draft-only brews and, perhaps, the annual Graffiti Wheat (a tribute to the locally-staged George Lucas movie "American Graffiti").

In order to help it weather turbulent times in the craft-brewing

RIGHT: *Would George Lucas prefer "SkywalkerWeizen" or "HefeJones"?*

industry, St. Stan's has undertaken contract work for several other producers. Purists may not like such a path, but the result allows the brewery to remain (St.) Stan–ding.

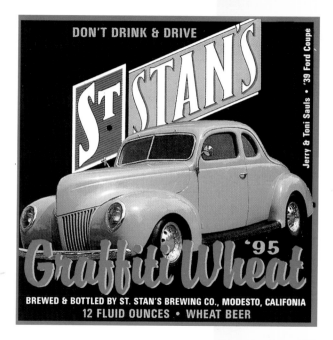

EST. 1996

155 Mata Way,
#104,
San Marcos,
California 92069
Tel: (760) 471 4999

RECOMMENDED
Stone Pale Ale
(5.4%), deep amber,
hoppy aroma and
bittering
Arrogant Bastard
(7.2%), reddish
mahogany, hopped
to the hilt!

STONE BREWING

The quality of Southern California's beer scene ramped up several notches with the opening of Stone Brewing. Ex-music business mavens Greg Koch and Steve Wagner teamed up to open their brewery in San Marcos, around 20 miles (32 km) north of San Diego. Their 30-barrel brewing system, large for a start-up, indicates their level of confidence in Stone Brewing's ales.

Stone Pale Ale is a complex amber ale, something of a cross between English and American styles, with delightful hop bitterness. Crafted from nearly 90 percent pale barley malt, it is full-bodied and slightly sweet; yet a blend of Nugget, Willamette, and Ahtanum hops give Stone Pale a zippy, balancing 45 BUs. The brewery also produces a collar-grabbing IPA, hopped to 65 BUs, and a balanced Smoked Porter (made with peat-smoked malt and aromatic Mt. Hood hops).

Their bière enfant terrible, how-ever, is an Arrogant Bastard. Liter-ally! This uncompromising brew has one of the most amusing labels in the beer industry (an industry not noted for label hilarity). Featuring a buff-muscled gargoyle holding a stein, the label proudly proclaims that the beer "isn't made for any sniveling yellow-beer-drinkin' wimps ... you're not worthy." Forget "soft" and "sub-tle" and get ready for a good slap in the palate. You've been warned.

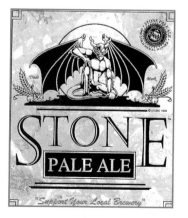

Named for the majestic Oregon peak, Mt. Hood hops are a Northwest relative of Germany's aromatic Hallertau hop.

277

EST. 1990
2001 Second Street,
Davis,
California 95616
Tel: (916) 753 2739

RECOMMENDED
Hübsch Pilsner
(5%), perhaps the
best in America
Hübsch Hefeweizen
(5.2%),
slightly light
interpretation of
Bavaria's best
Hübsch Märzen
(5.3%), rich,
creamy, layered
malt character

SUDWERK PRIVATBRAUEREI HÜBSCH

★

Another rare lager brewer in a sea of ales. Ron Broward founded the Hübsch brewpub (named after his mother's maiden name) to recapture the spirit of both the beers and friendly taverns of her German homeland. For authenticity, Broward installed a specially-made German brewhouse (or *sudhaus* in German) and employed a highly-experienced German brewmaster. Resulting demand for Hübsch's excellent German-style beers has had dual results: during 1996, the company opened both a new, fully-automated Steinecker brewery (approximately 20,000–barrel/23,500hl capacity) in Davis, as well as a second brewpub in California's capital, Sacramento

RIGHT: *Sudwerk's brewpub brings a taste of Germany to California's capital city.*

> The University of California at Davis trains many of America's new-generation brewers and (evenhandedly) winemakers.

(1375 Exposition Boulevard).

Five malts help give brewery flagship Hübsch Märzen a big body and complex character (balanced by classic German hops to 35 BUs). The Pilsner is elegant and refined with an outstanding floral aroma and bitterness from Hallertau, Spalt, and Tettnang hops. A delicate, fresh-tasting character sets Hübsch Pils apart from many "in-your-face" American interpretations of the style; look no farther for a true taste of Germany!

The brewery also crafts a Bavarian-style Hefeweizen, brewed with traditional estery Weihenstephan yeast, and a chocolatey Dunkel. Brewer David Sipes took over when Broward's German brewmaster departed in 1995, maintaining a beer legacy that still has fans jumping through "Hübsch." Stop by the pub and check out his (sud)werk.

RIGHT: *Measuring the progress of fermentation at Sudwerk Hübsch.*

Also worth trying

Northern California remains the state's "craft-beer cradle." Bay Area beerhunters should check out both the **Pyramid Ale Brewery** and **Golden Pacific Brewing**'s facility in Berkeley (just down the street from Pyramid). Golden Pacific – which merged with Berkeley's first craft-brewer, Thousand Oaks, in 1990 – offers its clean, honeyish Golden Bear Lager and nutty, hoppy Golden Gate Original Ale throughout the state. Just to the south of Berkeley, Oakland's **Pacific Coast** brewpub makes perhaps the finest malt-extract beers in the country.

In nearby San Leandro, the draft-only Lind Brewing offers up the dry-hopped Drake's Ale and its eponymous family: look for the deliciously-hoppy Drake's Gold and firm Sir Francis Stout, as well as specialties such as Drake's IPA (made with "extreme amounts of hops") and huge Jolly Roger's Holiday Ale. **Pete's Brewing** – the sizeable contract-brewer of Wicked Ale and other specialty beers, originally based across the bay in Palo Alto – faces an interesting future after being purchased in 1998 by the Texas-based Gambrinus company (see Southwest section).

Reports about **El Toro Brewing** in Morgan Hill are increasingly bullish. Try its Poppy Jasper ale. Eclectic drafts from Santa Rosa's **Moonlight Brewing** also have been gaining a Bay Area following (it's definitely not just a phase!).

Excellent microbreweries are becoming more prominent in the rest of the state. Sacramento's **Rubicon** brewpub, now open over ten years, serves well-respected beers that won't make you cross. Hollister's **San Andreas Brewing**, another veteran, makes pleasant (if not earth-shaking) ales, while Mt. Aukum's **El Dorado Brewing** earns praise for its hoppy Mountain Red Ale.

Just north of the San Francisco Bay Area is the town of Petaluma, home of **Lagunitas Brewing Co.** and its hoppy ales with delightful dog labels. Mix two for an "arf and arf!" Further north is a hot-bed of beer around the Eureka area. Seek out **Eel River Brewing**'s range (especially their rich black Ravensbrau porter) and the generously-hopped products from **Six Rivers** in McKinleyville.

In California's central valley town of Fresno, **Butterfield's Brewery** produces fine consistent products like their signature Tower Dark. On the coast near Santa Barbara, another winery-turned-brewer, **Firestone Walker**, is making its mark with interesting British-style brews (including an oak-fermented Double Barrel

Ale made with a version of England's rare "Burton Union" system).

The San Luis Obispo-based **SLO Brewing** – a brewpub known for its Olde Highland Ale and Cole Porter – took its time building a newly-opened $3.5 million production facility in the wine-booming town of Paso Robles (it still contract-brews its beers for east coast distribution, however). In the southern city of Irvine, **Steelhead Brewery** (a brewpub like its eponmous Oregon parent) pours distinctive beers, while regional micro **Bayhawk Ales** is more mainstream. In San Diego, two brewpubs named for German brewmaster **Karl Strauss** serve the best-known local suds.

Home to several local breweries and brewpubs, the city of Berkeley has billed itself as "the Napa Valley of Beer."

NORTHWEST

California may have started the craft brewing movement, but the Northwest – encompassing Oregon, Washington, Idaho, Montana, and Alaska – perfected it. Early micros such as Grant's, Redhook, BridgePort, Hale's, and Pyramid (who continue to thrive today) have been joined by many smaller producers. Portland, Oregon, hosts more breweries than any other North American city. The overall craft-beer market share in Oregon and Washington is at least five times the national average!

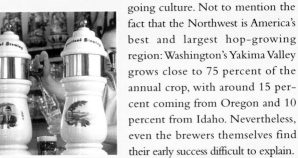

The success of Northwest craft-brewers can be attributed, in part, to passionate local support for "home grown" products. There's also the region's frequently-overcast climate, which fosters a pub-going culture. Not to mention the fact that the Northwest is America's best and largest hop-growing region: Washington's Yakima Valley grows close to 75 percent of the annual crop, with around 15 percent coming from Oregon and 10 percent from Idaho. Nevertheless, even the brewers themselves find their early success difficult to explain.

The prevalence of craft beer in the region means local competition is fierce. This is even more true after several of the Northwest's biggest specialty brewers, having experienced a lukewarm national reception for their beers, are refocusing attention on their home market. Still, Northwest drinkers continue to frequent the many "alehouses" (multi-tap pubs) serving their favorite brews.

EST. 1986
5429 Shaune Drive,
Juneau,
Alaska 99801
Tel: (907) 780 5866

RECOMMENDED
Alaskan
Frontier Amber
(4.5%), big bodied
but balanced
Alaskan
Smoked Porter
(6.2%), delicious,
if intense, blend
of flavors

ALASKAN BREWING

Brewing beer in Alaska isn't easy (which may explain why this upstart company is the state's oldest operating brewery). In the coastal community of Juneau, without road connections to the lower 48 states, everything arrives and leaves by water or air. For more than a decade now, a large part of the outbound cargo has been Alaskan Amber Ale – a smooth "alt" style beer based on a turn-of-the-century recipe from a brewery operating near Juneau during the gold rush era. It is offered year-round along with Alaskan Frontier and a notably fruity Pale Ale (dry-hopped). The addition of a new 100-barrel brewhouse in 1995 allowed Alaskan

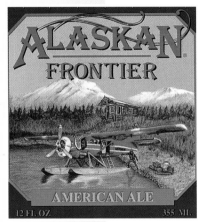

Brewing to dramatically increase production and distribution to serve the Northwest and northern California.

Flagship Alaskan Amber is amazingly popular, found in stores and bars throughout the region. The brewery has received greater critical acclaim, however, for its Smoked Porter and Alaskan Frontier. The former, brewed with grain cold-smoked over alder wood at a local Juneau fish smoker, has received five back-to-back gold medals at the Great American Beer Festival (fans cellar "vintages" for comparative tastings). Frontier, previously a seasonal called Autumn Ale, has been similarly rewarded in the Festival's "amber ale" category.

The year-round roll out of

Frontier – more distinctive than the regular Amber – marked an effort by Alaskan to "upgrade" its supporters' tastes. In 1998, the brewery took another step in this direction by introducing draft specialties such as an oily, roasty Oatmeal Stout. Impressed consumers are (Al)askin' for more!

RIGHT: *Getting ready for their trip south – bottles of Alaskan ales quench thirsts across the Pacific Northwest.*

1803 Presson Place,
Yakima,
Washington 98903
Tel: (509) 575 1900

RECOMMENDED
Scottish Ale
(4.7%), citrusy hop,
caramelized malt,
complex fruit
Fresh Hop Ale
(5.2%), resinous
hoppy flavor over
toasty malt
Imperial Stout
(6.6%), hoppy, roasty,
honeyish, rich

BERT GRANT'S ALES

★

Scottish-born Bert Grant entered the beer industry at Toronto's Canadian Breweries in 1945. Over the next 30 years, he worked for Stroh Breweries, Anheuser Busch, Coors, Guinness, and S.S. Steiner hops – ultimately becoming a top hop expert and joining Steiner at their Yakima headquarters. In 1982, Grant founded what's now the Northwest's oldest operating craft-brewery. Quickly realizing that free samples for visitors were hurting the bottom line, he turned it into America's first brew-pub since Prohibition. As a result of expansion, the brewery and Pub (32 North Front Street) now

RIGHT: *Northwest beer pioneer Bert Grant taps a cask of his acclaimed Scottish Ale to celebrate 15 years of brewing in 1997.*

BERT GRANT'S

Scottish Ale BRAND ™

A RICH, REAL ALE IN THE TRADITION
OF SCOTLAND; HOPPY IN THE
TRADITION OF YAKIMA.
BREWED AND BOTTLED BY
YAKIMA BREWING
MALTING CO., YAKIMA, WA
12 FL. OZ.

occupy separate locations. Production surpassed 20,000 barrels (23,500hl) in 1998, with semi-national distribution.

Grant's beers all show the character of his extremely estery ale yeast. The yeast's complex fruitiness works best in Grant's Scottish Ale and Imperial Stout, which are standard-bearers for the line. A golden India Pale Ale (launched in 1983) helped spark the style's rebirth with its American hops and then-unheard-of bitterness level (50 BUs). Other brews include a smoky, chocolatey Perfect Porter, mellow Amber Ale, and dry-hopped Glorious Golden Ale. Grant's four seasonal beers are each brewed with a single Yakima Valley hop variety: most unique is fall's Fresh Hop, seasoned with "green" Cascade hop blossoms taken directly from the harvesting fields to the brewery.

Tired of management issues — including a famous run-in with the Federal government over nutritional labeling on beer — Grant sold the brewery in 1995 to the company behind Washington's pioneering Chateau Ste. Michelle and Columbia Crest wineries. He remains active as brewmaster and founder.

RIGHT: *Introduced in 1982, Grant's Imperial Stout made a bold, powerful statement for beer early in the micro years.*

295

1313 NW Marshall,

EST. 1984
1313 NW Marshall,
Portland,
Oregon 97209
Tel: (503) 241 7179

RECOMMENDED
Blue Heron Ale
(4.9%), pleasant,
softly-malty
"session" quaffer
India Pale Ale
(5.5%), brightly
hoppy, fruity, and
quenching
Porter
(5.5%), creamy
and chocolatey, with
great balance

296

BRIDGEPORT BREWING

Oregon's oldest craft-brewery, BridgePort was founded by one of the most prominent families in the state's burgeoning wine industry. It is based, along with its comfortable pub, in a century-old brick building covered with climbing hop vines that stands in industrial northwest Portland. The company runs a second pub (no brewery), the BridgePort Ale House, on Hawthorne St. on the city's east side. Both locations serve cask-condi-

tioned versions of BridgePort beers. In 1995, BridgePort was purchased by the Gambrinus Company of Texas (see Southwest). Production in 1998 approached 25,000 barrels (29,300hl); distribution runs throughout the Northwest and west.

With Gambrinus' support, BridgePort has completed a $3.8 million overhaul and expansion program. This included the introduction of a new line of beers, launched with two keg- and bottle-condi-

Beers from BridgePort and Mendoncino Brewing both share the name "Blue Heron" by special agreement.

tioned ales: the exceptionally re-freshing, crisp, complex India Pale Ale (brewed with five hop varieties) and complex, smooth, balanced Porter. The range also includes a malty, estery ESB, sweetish Black Strap Stout (brewed with molasses), and "introductory" Amber Ale.

BridgePort heartened long-time fans with the 1998 relaunch – including new packaging and a reformulated recipe– of its original bottled beer, Blue Heron (Port-land's official city bird). The result is a surprisingly enjoyable, medium-bodied brew with a not-able Cascade hop aroma. BridgePort also has renewed commitment to Old Knucklehead (9.1%), its vintage-dated winter barleywine: viscous, rich in fruity esters, but drinkable even when young. Every year or so, the label features a new illustration of an actual Portland citizen who has been honored as the "knucklehead."

RIGHT: *Ivy, mixed with a couple of wandering hop vines, covers BridgePort's comfortable brewery pub in Portland.*

EST. 1988
901 SW Simpson,
Bend,
Oregon 97702
Tel: (503) 385 8606

RECOMMENDED
Mirror Pond
Pale Ale
(5%), cleanly fruity
with strong Cascade
character
Black Butte Porter
(5.6%), sweet,
smooth, and worth
seeking out
Obsidian Stout
(6.7%), richly chewy
and sweetish

DESCHUTES BREWERY

★

The city of Bend is one of Oregon's leading ski areas, viewed by many as the Northwest's finest. Deschutes is a leading regional brewery, also viewed by many as the Northwest's finest. Whatever your opinion, there's no question that Deschutes has advanced the cause of "dark beer" more than any other area craft-brewer. Its flag-

ship Black Butte Porter, creamy with notes of baker's chocolate and coffee, is the Northwest's best-selling example of the style; a mainstay on taps and shelves across the region.

Other rewarding year-round beers include

RIGHT: *Cones of silence?*
Only the hiss of fermenting
beer at Deschutes' production
facility in Bend.

Obsidian Stout, complex and potent in the "foreign" style, and Mirror Pond, a zestily-hopped west coast pale ale. Cascade Golden Ale displays an appealing, strongly grassy-citrusy hop character. The original Bachelor Bitter (perfect for jaded single men) has been revamped into the enhanced Bachelor ESB, offering rich nutty malt balanced by earthy East Kent Goldings hops. All of these beers, along with Black Butte, are bottle-conditioned.

Founded as a brewpub, Deschutes now operates a separate brewery whose capacity has increased to 84,000 barrels (98,500hl). The Deschutes Brewery & Public House (1044 NW Bond Street) still stands in Bend – its location even provides the name for the brewery's seasonal Bond Street Brown Ale, which is

available on draft only (as is summer's Paulina Pils). Winter's Jubelale (6.7%), in bottles and kegs, pairs a deep, candyish malt character with heapin' helpings of Northwest hops; it sometimes is dispensed with nitrogen for extra-creamy character. Distribution is widespread in the Northwest, California, and Hawaii.

RIGHT: *Deschutes' brewhouse is clean and well-made, just like the beers that flow from its shapely vessels.*

EST. 1987
506 Columbia,
Hood River,
Oregon 97031
Tel: (541) 386 2281

RECOMMENDED
Equinox ESB
(5.7%), rich malt,
tangy zesty hop
Amber Ale
(6%), a malt bomb
before hoppy finish
Imperial Porter
(7%), huge, warming
interpretation
of style

FULL SAIL BREWING

Full Sail is located at the end of a truly "gorgeous" drive from Portland, along the scenic Columbia River Gorge. Hood River's main claim to fame is its suitability for windsurfing – sail-boarders take full advantage of gusty winds swooping down where the Hood River meets the Columbia. Their activity inspired the name of the brewery, which was founded by a former wine salesman.

The current facility, with a pub overlooking the Gorge, is housed in an old fruit-packing plant. Its impressive new brewhouse, capable of expansion up to 250,000 barrels (293,350hl), is supplemented by a smaller "brewpub" facility in Portland (The Riverplace Brewery, 0307 SW Montgomery, 97201). Full Sail beers are widely available throughout the west.

Full Sail's classic Amber is big-bodied, malty, and deep, balanced at the finish with Cascade and Mt. Hood hops. It is joined year-round

A tribute to Northwest tastes, Amber quickly overtook Full Sail's original golden ale after its introduction.

305

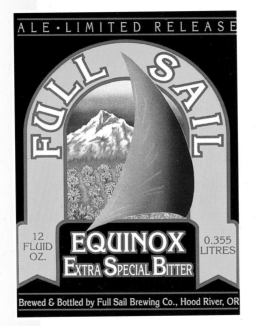

by the sharply-citrusy Very Special Pale Ale (introduced as a 10th Anniversary brew) and toffee-chocolatey Nut Brown Ale. Full Sail's line of seasonals includes a pleasant Oktoberfest lager and summertime IPA (brewed with three pounds of East Kent Goldings per barrel). Spring's ESB bursts with fresh hop character from English Target and Saaz varieties, while January's impenetrable Imperial Porter skillfully manages to elevate the style in all aspects while avoiding stout territory. A separate hearty winter warmer called WasSail (get it?) is chewy and candyish with a spicy-hop kick – it perfectly illustrates Full Sail's slogan, "Big Beers for real beer lovers."

EST. 1994
4509 SE 23rd,
Portland,
Oregon 97202
Tel: (503) 236 3555

RECOMMENDED
Golden Rose
(7.5%), fruity,
warming, with subtle
hop profile
Adam beer
(10%), rich,
complex, almost
whiskey-ish

HAIR OF THE DOG BREWING

★

If Full Sail crafts "big beers," then Hair of the Dog must brew giants. This tiny micro has an amusing name and slogan – "Faithful, Loyal, Pure, Wet Nose" – but its ales are incredibly serious: potent, bottle-conditioned, and designed to improve with age. Each bottle is labeled with the brew's batch-number for easy reference. Production is extremely limited, yet distribution includes the west coast and a few eastern regions.

Golden Rose, made with special honey-malt and candy sugar, is styled after a Belgian Tripel. Adam beer, the original brew, is an attempt to reproduce a well-aged strong ale reportedly once popular in Dortmund, Germany. Two-year-old bottles of Adam show no signs of sluggishness, but rather are

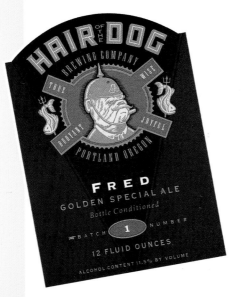

hugely complex – notes of rich malt, tropical fruits, peat smoke, chocolate, and coffee – and eminently satisfying. Adventurous drinkers should get hold of a case, store it properly, and wait to see what develops.

In 1997, Hair of the Dog introduced "Fred," a yet-stronger (11.5%) brew designed in honor of Portland-based beer writer and homebrewer Fred Eckhardt. Brewed with ten hop varieties from five different countries, along with a portion of rye malt, this deep golden ale drinks far too easily for its potency. Fred's second runnings are used to make the draft-only "Ed," a more quaffable version. (Of course, for Hair of the Dog, "more quaffable" means just over five percent by volume).

RIGHT: *Hair of the Dog founders Alan Sprints (left) and Doug Henderson (right) flank beer critic Michael Jackson (center).*

311

HALE'S ALES

★

EST. 1983
4301 Leary Way NW,
Seattle,
Washington 98107
Tel: (206) 706 1544

RECOMMENDED
Moss Bay Extra
(4.6%), rich nutty malt
meets Northwest hops

O'Brien's
Harvest Ale
(4.8%), famously
hoppy copper-
colored seasonal

Moss Bay Stout
(5.4%), smooth,
sweetish, creamy

In the early 1980s, Mike Hale's passion for British beer led him to work at Gale's brewery in Hampshire, England. Armed with his experience and some Gale's yeast, he returned to Washington and built a brewery (out of used dairy equipment) near the city of Spokane. Driven by the slogan "Give 'em Hale's," his beers benefited from early interest in microbrews. Production shifted to a site in Spokane proper before Hale's established a second facility near Seattle. The current Seattle headquarters, opened in 1995, features a new brewhouse – complete with English-inspired open fermenters – and an integrated pub. It now handles all production since Hale's Spokane

312

brewery was moth-
balled in 1998.

Hale's success
sounds pretty
straightforward
until you realize
that the company
only sold draft beer
for its first 15
years. Today, a bottled
range includes versions
of the Pale Ale, Amber
Ale, and Moss Bay Extra

(named after the location of the company's first Seattle-area brewery). Unfortunately all seem to lose something in the transition from draft. Kegs remain the best containers for the robust Celebration Porter and seasonals such as O'Brien's Harvest and a wintertime Wee Heavy (spiced with cinnamon). Taps are also the place to find Hale's "Dublin-style" brews, dispensed with nitrogen: these range from a Boddingtons-like Cream Ale and mellow Hale's Special Bitter (HSB) to the more interesting Stout. Distribution mainly encompasses western Washington and Oregon.

BELOW: *Ready to "hop" into action,*
Hale's "Emergency Beer Delivery Unit"
waits to save another thirsty customer.

EST. 1989
140 Lakeside Avenue,
Suite 300,
Seattle,
Washington 98122
Tel: (206) 322 5022

RECOMMENDED
Pale Ale
(4.5%), rich nutty malt,
balancing earthy hops
**XXXXX Pike
Street Stout**
(6%), espresso roast,
rich chocolate,
assertive hops
India Pale Ale
(6.2%), seriously
hoppy, bitter over
thick malt

PIKE BREWING

★

An English-inspired brewery founded by Charles Finkel, whose Merchant du Vin company imports Samuel Smith's ales and other classic European beers. Its tiny original facility (with a four-and-a-half barrel brewkettle) stood six floors below Seattle's Pike Place Market. This plant has been replaced by the nearby Pike Pub and Brewery (1415 First Avenue), which opened in 1996. With its dramatically increased capacity (15,000 barrels/17,600hl), the new brewery came as a relief to thirsty regional fans. In

RIGHT: *Pike's new brewhouse dwarfs its original cramped quarters beneath Seattle's Pike Place Market.*

Pike's Seattle pub contains a "brewery museum" with items illustrating the region's micro-brewing history.

addition, after years of contract arrangements, all of Pike's beers now are brewed at its Seattle home. Distribution is best throughout California and the greater Northwest region.

Despite its small size, the original Pike Place Brewery had a hugely positive reputation – the result of Finkel's creative marketing and brewer Fal Allen's excellent British-

style ales. Floor-malted Maris Otter barley, imported from England, imparts a wonderfully rich flavor to Pike's Pale Ale. The deep-copper IPA balances its chewy maltiness with loads of Chinook, Golding, and Willamette hops. These two beers are available year-round.

Pike also supplies specialties such as winter's spiced Auld Acquaintance and the hearty Old Bawdy barleywine (a reference to the original brewery's location, the site of a former brothel). The "five-X" Stout, offering pots of coffee-roast character over rich, mouthfilling maltiness, appears during cooler seasons. Kilt Lifter, Allen's moderately-hoppy take on a Scotch ale, looks set to become a year-round beer thanks to its initial popularity. A Saaz-hopped Golden Ale, light-bodied Porter, and several other rotating beers also are produced.

EST. 1986
2730 NW 31st
Avenue,
Portland,
Oregon 97210
Tel: (503) 226 7623

**RECOMMENDED
MacTarnahan's
Amber Ale**
(5%), toasty
malt, toffee;
moderate body

PORTLAND BREWING

★

Portland Brewing's original brewpub (1339 NW Flanders, 97209) still produces draft specialties in the shadow of the city's large Blitz–Weinhard Brewery—in fact, its space has been expanded. But standard production now comes from the showplace facility on industrial NW 31st Avenue. Inside, the brewery's welcoming tap room adjoins a classic copper brewhouse purchased from the Sixenbräu Brewery in Bavaria. Its vessels provide a fitting birthplace for Portland's filtered Bavarian-style Weizen, available at the pub and in select markets.

RIGHT: *A shiny mash tun and kettle are the centerpieces of Portland's copper-and-tile brewhouse.*

Portland's annual production now approaches 60,000 barrels (70,400hl); growth has been funded through a series of stock offerings. Among its core brands, MacTarnahan's Amber Ale (malt accented in the "Scottish style") offers an extremely balanced example of the style with absolutely no rough edges; it's a quaffer. Same goes for the Zig Zag River Lager, burnished-golden in color with a solid mouthfeel and peppery, hoppy finish.

The brewery's year-round range also includes an almost-opaque Haystack Black Porter (with a bitter-roast finish) and clean-tasting, sweetish Oregon Honey Beer that – for a while, anyway – was the darling of southern California drinkers. Summer Ale, made with brewery-distilled hop oil to en-

hance its aroma, was supposedly inspired by the original, Northwest-hopped Portland Ale (now sadly discontinued). Winter's Icicle Creek, warming and sweetish again, is more substantial and better known. Portland's ales are available across the west and in a handful of eastern markets.

RIGHT: *Portland's Zig Zag River lager here follows a smooth curve down the brewery's bottling line.*

PYRAMID BREWERIES

EST. 1984
91 S. Royal
Brougham, Seattle,
Washington 98134
Tel: (206) 682 8322

RECOMMENDED
Pyramid Espresso
Stout (5.6%),
mouthfilling mix of
coffee, chocolate,
hops
Pyramid India
Pale Ale
(6.7%), sweet malt
body, intense hops
Pyramid Snow
Cap Ale
(6.9%), robust,
beautifully-balanced
"winter warmer"
324

Pyramid was founded in a small Washington logging town relatively close to Portland, Oregon. The company later acquired Thomas Kemper Brewing, a pioneering lager-producing micro (originally based on the Kitsap Peninsula across Puget Sound from Seattle). Today, production of both brands, as well as Kemper's specialty sodas (root beer, etc.), is divided between the company's two newer breweries: its Seattle headquarters (near the downtown sports stadiums) and $14.5 million California expansion, the Pyramid Brewery & Alehouse (901 Gilman, Berkeley, 94710).

Pyramid's push for mainstream appeal with "user-friendly" brews – its original (filtered) Wheaten Ale, clean-tasting Hefeweizen, über-

RIGHT: *Berkeley or Beer-kly? Thomas Kemper tie-dies? It will be tough for Pyramid to top its $14.5 million brewery in the Bay Area's counter-culture capital.*

Pyramid used to
change the hops
in Snowcap Ale
each year. Purists
want this worth-
while tradition
reinstated

fruity Apricot Ale, and soft ESB – is tempered by the retention of classics such as the robust Snow Cap and coffeeish but caffine-free Espresso Stout (sometimes dispensed with nitrogen). And while Pyramid Pale Ale has lost hoppiness – now approaching the mellowness of its nitrogen counterpart, Draught Pale Ale (DPA) – the lupulin banner is carried by a delightfully Columbus-stuffed IPA. Spring's rich Scotch Ale and summer's peppery dry-hopped Sun Fest lager (based on the original Thomas Kemper Pilsner) are also worth seeking out.

In recent years, the Kemper beers have played second fiddle to Pyramid's. In 1998, a facelift for the line included the introduction of new packaging and "homey" names for the creamy Half-Ton Hefeweizen and grainy, unfiltered Auction Block Amber ale. Kemper's most distinctive beers remain seasonal lagers such as its dark bock-like Winter-Bräu, spring's golden Bock, and nutty, hoppy Oktoberfest.

Pyramid Ales are available throughout the west and select other American markets, with Kemper's distribution limited mainly to the Northwest and California. Pyramid Breweries went public in 1996.

RIGHT: *Although a filtered Wheaten Ale drove Pyramid's early success, today's flagship is yeasty Hefeweizen.*

327

REDHOOK ALE BREWERIES

★

ESTABLISHED 1982

3400 Phinney Avenue N., Seattle, Washington 98103 Tel: (206) 548 8000

RECOMMENDED
Redhook Rye
(5%), unfiltered and refreshingly tangy

One of the best-known names in craft-brewing. Redhook's Seattle brewery, located in an old brick "trolley barn," was shuttered in 1998 – though its Trolley-man Pub and company offices remain. The goal was to maximize production at two newer facilities: Woodinville, Washington (14300 NE 145th Street, 98072)

and Portsmouth, New Hampshire (35 Corporate Drive, Pease International Tradeport, 03801). Redhook went public in 1996 and trades on Nasdaq. Following a path sharply different from similarly-

RIGHT: *All smiles at the largest craft-brewery in the Pacific Northwest (not to mention New England).*

successful brewers such as Sierra Nevada and Anchor, Redhook exemplifies a course feared by many craft-beer aficionados. As the company's volume and distribution have increased – driven in part by a far-reaching deal with Anheuser-Busch (which owns 25 percent equity in the Seattle-based brewer) – the character of its beers seems to have been "toned down." Nowhere is the result more evident than in the flagship Extra Special Bitter. Once full of fruity, malty, hoppy flavors, Redhook ESB now is a mellow amber ale with smooth toffee, butterscotch notes. Redhook's super-clean Hefeweizen (in the Northwest style), summer Blonde Ale, and buttery IPA also exemplify this trend.

More flavor remains in the roasty Blackhook Porter and yet-roastier, bitter Double Black Stout (brewed with Seattle's famous Starbucks coffee). Redhook's pioneering

Rye, with is sharply-spicy grain-
iness, is a worthwhile quencher –
yet apparently in danger of being
discontinued. The seasonal Winter-
hook, once a standout in its own
right, now offers a taste of the ESB's
original character. Long-time supporters still hope that Redhook will
reclaim its distinctive brewing roots.

RIGHT: *In the beer garden at Redhook's*
Woodinville brewery, located within
spitting distance of Columbia winery.

EST. 1988
2320 OSU Drive,
Newport,
Oregon 97365
Tel: (541) 867 3660

RECOMMENDED
Mogul Ale
(6.5%), chewy,
chocolatey,
powerfully hoppy
Imperial Stout
(11%), deep and
deceptively smooth
Old Crustacean
(11.3%), hugely
fruity-hoppy
barley wine

ROGUE ALES

A small Oregon coast fishing town seems an unlikely home for this aggressive craft-brewer. The company is named after Oregon's Rogue River, but its moniker also encapsulates both the brewery's philosophy and the colorful personality of its founder Jack Joyce. A broad range of traditional and exotic-nouveau ales is offered; many illustrate head brewer John Maier's passion for citric Northwest hops. Rogue's Brutal Bitter is packed with the relatively-new Crystal variety (to 59 BUs), for example, while the Imperial India Pale Ale (I^2PA) refreshes palates with a powerful punch of Cascades, Goldings, and Saaz.

Rogue's take-no-prisoners attitude comes off best in its bigger beers. Old Crustacean, legendarily hoppy when fresh, turns mellow and finessed with a few years' age. A portion of rolled oats makes the bold, rich Imperial Stout — as well as the complex Shakespeare Stout, easier

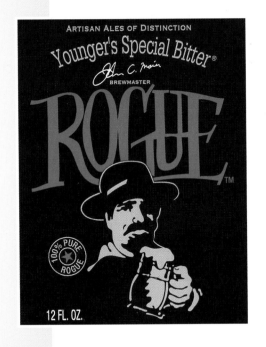

to find and equally outstanding – deceptively drinkable. Both "Old Crusty" and the Imperial are sold in seven-ounce bottles as part of Rogue's XS Series, along with the (I^2PA) and McRogue Scotch Ale. Mogul Ale, the winter seasonal, shines on draft.

Opinions divide on several of the brewery's other offerings – a hazelnut-flavored brown ale, light Honey Cream Ale, Younger's Special Bitter (named for famous Portland publican Don Younger), and Artisan Amber lager – as well as its practice of selling the same beer under many different labels (Dead Guy, anyone?). But Rogue really doesn't care about other people's opinions. Rogue Ales are available in more than 30 states, with 1997 production nearing 20,000 barrels (23,500hl).

RIGHT: *Give me liberty or give me …
lager? Rogue's foray out of ale territory
has met with a mixed reception.*

EST. 1993
5875 SW Lakeview
Blvd., Lake Oswego,
Oregon 97035
Tel: (503) 699 9524

RECOMMENDED
Nor'Wester Oregon
Pale Ale
(5.5%), complex
citrusy hops, smooth
nutty malt
Saxer Bock
(7.2%), copper color,
smooth, spicily-
hopped
Jack Frost
(8.0%), satiatingly
rich, malty

SAXER BREWING

★

Located in a Portland suburb, Saxer took its name – as well as its focus on German-style lager beers – from the German immigrant who opened one of Oregon's first breweries in the 1850s. Difficult financial circumstances in the early years were off-set by the success of Saxer's light, shandy-like Lemon Lager (critic-ally drubbed, publicly loved). Today, brew-master Tony Gomes, who attended brewing school and apprenticed in Bavaria, crafts more-traditional beers in his decoction brewhouse.

Saxer bets its brewing dollars on bock beers, for which it deservedly has collected several medals at the Great American Beer Festival. The

Saxer hangs its hat on bock beers, for which it has won several medals at the annual Great American Beer Festival.

year-round *helles* (pale) Saxer Bock is joined by spring's vinous red-brown Dark Bock and winter's still-richer, Salvator-esque Jack Frost doppelbock. All possess a creaminess of character that comes from extended lagering. A full-bodied Pilsner, with strong hop presence, was introduced in summer 1998. The company also still offers a line of "Three Finger Jack" beers (named for an Oregon outlaw), such as a caramel-accented Hefedunkel dark lager.

In 1997, Saxer acquired the rights to brands and recipes from Portland's bankrupt Nor'Wester Brewing (including a straightforward Hefeweizen and candyish Raspberry Weizen). In addition to repackaging the line with striking labels by an Oregon photographer, Saxer launched a surprisingly-distinctive Nor'Wester brew, Oregon Pale Ale (a crisply-hoppy beer in the best Northwest tradition). Saxer also has continued Nor'Wester's sponsorship of an annual Portland homebrewing competition. Saxer and Nor'Wester beers are available in the Northwest and select other markets.

RIGHT: *The Saxer crew surrounds medal-winning (and wearing) brewmaster Tony Gomes during the 1997 holidays.*

339

EST. 1984
929 N. Russell Street,
Portland,
Oregon 97227
Tel: (503) 281 2437

RECOMMENDED
Hop Jack Pale Ale
(5%), sweet, toasty
malt; lingering
citrusy hop
Altbier
(4.9%), big malt
body, spicy
German hops

WIDMER BROTHERS BREWING

The house that Hefeweizen built. The original Altbier experienced moderate success, but founding brothers Kurt and Rob Widmer saw demand explode after they introduced an unfiltered version in 1986: it quickly metamorphosed into top-selling Widmer Hefeweizen, the pioneering unfiltered American-style wheat ale. With its approachable yeasty flavor and distinctive cloudy appearance (usually enhanced with a slice of lemon on the glass), Widmer Hefeweizen converted scores of Northwest

drinkers to craft-beer.

In 1996, fueled by Hefeweizen's success, Widmer supplemented its original brewery and on-site pub (the "Gasthaus") with a new 250-barrel Huppmann brewhouse whose potential annual capacity approaches 750,000 barrels (880,000hl).

341

(Talk about a "hefe-duty" facility!). A year later, following the footsteps of Washington's Redhook, Widmer entered into an alliance with Anheuser-Busch –trading a "minority" interest for access to the mega-brewer's distribution network. Production in 1998 topped 120,000 barrels (140,800hl), with distribution across the west and select Midwest and east coast markets.

In addition to Hefeweizen, Widmer's year-round beers include a clean-tasting Pilsner and creamy Big Ben Porter brewed with licorice and molasses. The unfiltered Hop Jack Pale Ale, presenting plenty of Centennial hop character, and original Altbier (on draft around Portland) are more notable. On the seasonal front, watch for the refreshing, subtle Sommerbrau (modeled on a Kölsch) and winter's chocolatey draft-only Doppelbock (7.3%). In 1998, Kurt and Rob rolled out samples of a dark, robust Bourbon Bock (10%) matured in used whisky barrels. Hopefully such distinctive experiments will set the tone for Widmer's brewing future.

RIGHT: *The cathedral of brewing: Widmer's new über-capacity brewhouse takes up a beerhall's worth of space.*

Also worth trying

As far north and west as possible, Alaska offers tasty options for thirsty tundra-tamers. Anchorage houses the **Bird Creek** and **Midnight Sun** breweries: look for the former's crisply-hopped Old 55 Pale Ale and Alaskafest holiday beer; the latter crafts a "thick and woolly" Mammoth Extra Stout and creative "Three-Barrel" line of specialties. The city also is home to several brewpubs. In 1998, the **Silver Gulch** brewery opened outside of Fairbanks.

Washington hosts several other craft-brewers making interesting beers. Salmon Bay Bitter from Seattle's **Maritime Pacific** is a satisfying example of the traditional British style. Serious drinkers watch for powerful IPAs from Mukilteo's tiny **Diamond Knot Brewery** and North Bend's **Snoqualmie Falls Brewing** (now home to ex Thomas Kemper brewmaster Rande Reed). Carved cowboy tap-handles denote ales from northern **Winthrop Brewing**, including the punny Hop-Along Red. Seattle bars and restaurants offer plenty of choices for sampling: try the Nickerson Street Saloon (318

"Brewed in the Northwest with Imagination"

Nickerson) in the Fremont district.

Savvy drinkers in capital city Olympia catch fresh Fish Tale Ales, such as the mocha-like Mud Shark Porter and bold IPA, at the local **Fishbowl** brewpub; elsewhere, scout for the beers in bottles and on tap. Heading east, German-themed **Leavenworth** hosts an eponymous micro making aggressive ales and lagers. The Yakima Valley now houses **Cirque Brewery** and its line of "triple-mashed" lagers, while Tri-Cities tapsters pour ales from Pasco's **Ice Harbor Brewing**. Heading east, Montana finally is flood-ing with small producers. Look for a nutty Doppelbock from revitalized **Kessler Brewing**, a firm Pilsener from **Bayern Brewing**, and the Tri-Motor Amber from **Lang Creek Brewing**.

In Oregon, thirsty Portlanders go to the dogs at the **Lucky Labrador** brewpub and wet their whistle with the hoppy-fruity Red Thistle from McMinnville's **Golden Valley Brewery**. At the end of every July, Portland's outdoor Oregon Brewers Festival puts the region's best on tap. Otherwise, head for the Rose & Raindrop (532 Southeast Grand) or

345

another of the city's many pubs. To the south, Eugene's **Steelhead** and **Wild Duck** brewpubs offer a range of adventurous beers. Farther east, in the prosaic town of Government Camp on the south slope of Mt. Hood, well-hopped ales are crafted by **Mt. Hood Brewing**. Even non-climbers will enjoy the Ice Axe IPA, Pinnacle ESB, appropriately rich Pittock Wee Heavy, and satisfying Hogsback Oatmeal Stout (made with molasses and licorice). Closer to the California border, **Wild River Brewing** of Grant's Pass offers a selection of distinctive brews: try the rich caramel ESB and "lower octane" Imperial Stout.

A "bitter" choice: today, more than 30 different hop varieties grow in the Northwest's fields.

CANADA WEST

The phrase "Canada West" evokes images of Vancouver and other Pacific coastal cities, or perhaps of all British Columbia itself. But in specialty beer terms, Canada West encompasses British Columbia eastward through Manitoba. In general, both the Pacific and Prairie craft-brews of Canada share a broadly similar character (malt-accented, "soft") that separates them from more aggressively-flavorful ales and lagers that are found in the eastern regions.

The best example of this "western" character is McNally's Ale, a supremely malty Irish-styled ale produced by Alberta's Big Rock Brewery. Even in Vancouver, only three hours' drive from super-hoppy Seattle, the majority of microbrews – from Shaftebury Cream Ale to Granville Island's soft Pale Ale – remain malt-accented. Nevertheless, there are exceptions: Vancouver's Storm Brewing, Squamish's Tall Ship Ales, and North Vancouver's Sailor Hägar's Brewery all offer India Pale Ales that speak directly to the style's super-hopped roots.

It is mainly western brewers who gather each November at the Great Canadian Beer Festival in Victoria, British Columbia. Sponsored by the Canadian branch of Britain's Campaign for Real Ale, the event offers a convenient way to get a taste of Canada's westerly craft-brewing industry.

EST. 1994
9929 – 60 Avenue,
Edmonton,
Alberta T6E 0C7
Tel: (403) 436-8922

RECOMMENDED
Aprikat
(4.1%), notably
refreshing, quaffable
fruit beer
Olde Deuteronomy
(10.5%), a chocolate-
cherry winter warmer

ALLEY KAT BREWING

★

The city of Edmonton may be surrounded by arable farmland, but Alberta's capital has proven to be far from fertile ground for craft breweries. Alley Kat Brewing is a successful exception proving the rule. Production capacity at the brewery approached 3,600 barrels (4,200hl) in 1998, with distribution limited to the Alberta area.

Bucking the trend that had seen the rise and demise of many a small Edmonton brewery, homebrewers Neil Herbst and Richard Cholon (who has since left the company) founded Alley Kat with an eye on shaking up the generally moribund local beer scene. That they did, but only after they replaced their original beer line-up of an amber lager and

a wheat ale with a much more experimental group – "Real Beer For Kool Kats," boast labels – that includes everything from fruit beers to a barley wine. The one exception is Redneck Beer, a brew styled for the audience its names suggests.

Two fruit beers form the base of Alley Kat's portfolio: the apricot-based Aprikat and the raspberry-flavored Razzy Kat.

Brewer Herbst also produces Alberta's hoppiest beer, the citrusy, nutty Full Moon Pale Ale; a commercially-oriented Scona Gold Cream Ale; the quaffable, toasty Alley Kat Amber; and a robust, malty barley wine in the British style, Olde Deuteronomy. Alley Kat beers also sport some of the most attractive labels in western Canada, each one featuring a fanciful piece of feline-themed art.

EST. 1985

6403 – 35 Street SE,
Calgary,
Alberta T2C 1N2
Tel: (403) 279 2917

RECOMMENDED

Warthog Ale
(5%), nutty, toffee
flavors with
balancing hop

Black Amber Ale
(5%), pleasantly rich,
mocha-y and smooth

McNally's Ale
(7%), deeply complex
and thoroughly
rewarding

BIG ROCK BREWERY

★

The largest ale-only craft brewer in Canada, Big Rock was founded by former lawyer Edward McNally, who became interested in brewing after retiring to a farm and serving as director of a Canadian barley growers' association. Sales grew steadily (if slowly) at first, but were aided by the 1987 introduction of

McNally's Ale and the foothold it gave the company in the American micro market. In 1997, Big Rock replaced all of its existing brewing facilities – including two expanded-site buildings named Bigger Rock and Big Big Big Rock, respectively – with a completely new plant on the edge of Calgary (ultimately capable of producing

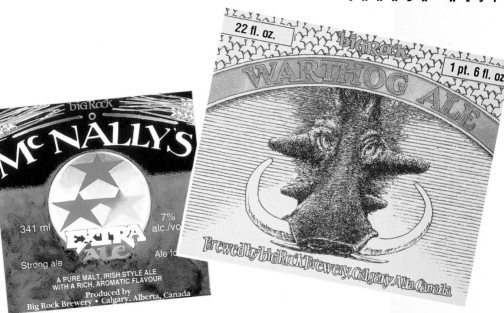

383,500barrels/450,000hl per year). Distribution is widespread throughout the United States and Canada. The company trades publicly on Canada's Alberta and Toronto Stock Exchanges and America's Nasdaq.

Big Rock brews several year-round beers, including a pleasantly malty Traditional Ale, the strong, bittersweet Black Amber Ale (a kind of strong porter), the pioneering (for Canada, anyway) Magpie

Rye Ale, the more complex Warthog, and tame Grasshöpper Wheat (the best thing about it is the umlaut). The star of the Big Rock show, however, is McNally's Ale, brewed in the "Irish style." Orange-amber in color, with a mouthfilling, smooth, deep malt character and balancing toasty-bitter flavor, it ranks among the most rewarding beers brewed in North America.

EST. 1994
3300 Bridgeway St.,
Vancouver,
B.C. V5K 1H9
Tel: (604) 293-2282

RECOMMENDED
Special Bitter
(4.5%), dark
malt character with
notable hops
Harvest Ale
(4.5%), brewed
with fresh-harvested
Mt. Hood hops

BOWEN ISLAND BREWERY

This brewery began life as a tiny operation on the eponymous island, accessible from the British Columbia mainland only via the Horseshoe Bay ferry. Now occupying new mainland premises, Bowen beers are distributed around the province in bottles and kegs, with its strongest representation in Vancouver. Four year-round beers are offered, including the flagship Bowen Ale (a sweetish pale ale lightly balanced by American hops) and Blonde Ale (brewed with 25 percent wheat malt). Brewed in the mild "Canadian ale" style, Bowen Blonde may be British Columbia's best cross-over beer: it will "make a lager drinker swoon," according to *Vancouver Magazine*.

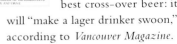

Bowen's third always-available beer is Special Bitter: richer, maltier, and hoppier – thanks to Cascades, Goldings, and Mt. Hoods – than the standard Canadian craft-brewed "British ale." The brewery's fourth and most recent offering is the phenomenally successful Original Hemp Cream Ale, launched in the spring of 1998 to widespread interest and corresponding sales. It is characterized by an intriguing mix of fruit and spice, including notes of caraway and cumin in the body, and a decidedly creamy mouthfeel. Bowen's seasonal Harvest Ale, malty-toasty and smooth, is followed by a Winter Ale – formerly brewed as a cherry-flavored dry stout!

In the spring of 1998, Bowen purchased the struggling, Asian market-driven Coquihalla Brewery and now produces its range of more mainstream lagers.

A move to the mainland has raised Bowen Island's profile and helped expand the market for its ales.

EST. 1984

1441 Cartwright St,
Vancouver,
B.C. V6H 3R7

Tel: (604) 687 2739

RECOMMENDED
Brockton Black
Lager
(6.5%), smooth,
chocolate-licorice
malt character

Seasonal
Prototap
(varies), ongoing
line of limited
specialties

GRANVILLE ISLAND

C anada's original micro – the first free-standing microbrewery to open in the country. The name came from its location, Granville Island, a thriving creative community located in the heart of Vancouver. The Island's waterfront markets bustle with artisans, craftspeople, and the tourists that come to admire them. Founder Mitchell Taylor chose the site for its colorful character and proximity to the thirsty Vancouver market.

Despite its pride of place in Canadian micro-

RIGHT: *Granville Island's operation in Vancouver houses a pilot brewery and retail shop.*

mythology, the brewery has a check-ered business history: it merged with an energy company in 1985, then was purchased in 1989 by a distill-ery company that also owned older regional Pacific Western Brewing. The distillery group, now known as Cascadia Brands, retains control of Granville Island Brewing and has moved the brewing facilities to the com-pany's home base of Kelowna, B.C. At the same time, new packaging was introduced to empha-size the brewery's Vancouver roots.

The Granville Island location now houses an impressive hospitality/ beer education center and a small-scale brewery where brewer Mark Simpson develops Granville's new line of specialty beers under the Seasonal Prototap banner (available at the Island brewery and select B.C. Liquor

Stores). Granville Island's main brands include the original, flagship Island Lager (a balanced Bavarian-style helles), the soft English Bay Pale Ale, and fuller-bodied Gastown Amber Ale. Brockton Black Lager (formerly the Island Bock) is the most distinctive, with a smooth, rich (chocolatey?) flavor and softly warming finish. A rich Scotch Ale and suitably fruity Apricot Alt have ranked among the most impressive Prototap beers.

ENGLISH BAY
pale ale

5% ALC./VOL.   HANDCRAFTED 1516 ALL NATURAL   341 mL

EST. 1994
86 Semisch Avenue,
North Vancouver,
B.C. V7M 3H8
Tel: (604) 984 3087

RECOMMENDED
Lohin's ESB
(5.6%), toasty malt,
caramel hints,
hoppy finish
India Pale Ale
(6.5%), probably
B.C.'s best
hophead beer
Thor's Barley Wine
(12%), the heft of the
god's hammer

SAILOR HÄGAR'S BREWERY & PUB

A pub that became a brewpub that became a microbrewery. Sailor Hägar's is accessible via "sea bus" ferry across Burrard Inlet from downtown Vancouver. It is worth the trip for the pub alone, which provides an enjoyable English-style setting and a spectacular view of the Vancouver skyline. The brewery itself is a compact, stainless steel affair tucked in a small building up the road (talk about long beer lines!). Between the two is Sailor Hägar's Beer & Wine Shop, which offers PET-bottle six-packs of the company's beers in addition to a wide range of west coast craft-brands (from America and Canada).

Sailor Hägar's brewmaster Gary Lohin makes respectable lagers, including a vaguely Märzen-styled "Scandinavian Amber." But Lohin's adventurous skills show best in ales

such as his extremely drinkable ESB: served through a hand-pump, it has a smooth, creamy mouthfeel with toasty malt notes, a solidly hoppy character, and a dry, hoppy finish. A seasonal (late fall) IPA bursts with citric American hops and would be perfectly at home at any Seattle or Portland alehouse.

Lohin's "highly coriandered" Belgian Wit, while less balanced, still marks a creative departure from the British Columbia norm. Other occasional specialties have included a lightly-peated Wee Heavy, a Northwest-hoppy Columbus Pale Ale, and an intense yet balanced Thor's Barley Wine. Unfortunately for downtown and south suburban Vancouverites, B.C. laws at present prevent Sailor Hägar's from selling their beer beyond their own taps and beer shop.

Sailor Hägar's truly is a "jewel" in Vancouver's bar and beer scene.

EST. 1994
39002 E. Discovery
Way, Squamish,
B.C. V0N 3G0
Tel: (604) 892-5696

RECOMMENDED
India Pale Ale
(7.5%), massive
fruitiness and great
complexity
**Russian
Imperial Stout**
(9.5%), fabulously
complicated, delight
for the palate
No. 1 Barley Wine
(11.2%), flavorful,
drinkable "boozy
spice cake"

TALL SHIP ALE COMPANY

In today's dynamic market, craft-breweries sometimes must reinvent themselves in pursuit of success. Just ask Bill Herdman, co-founder of Tall Ship Ales.

Over the past four-plus years, Herdman frequently has altered the look and even the taste of Tall Ship's beers. Early on, for example, Tall Ship ran afoul of

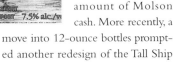

national giant Molson, who thought the small brewery's logo was too similar to the ship on its Molson Export label. An out-of court settlement saw Tall Ship change its design in exchange for a not-insignificant amount of Molson cash. More recently, a move into 12-ounce bottles prompted another redesign of the Tall Ship line. The one constant, however, has been quality: no matter what brewer Herdman has developed, Tall Ship beers have always been clean, complex and full of flavor.

The latest, and hopefully final, incarnation of Tall Ship features four impressive, bottle-conditioned ales. The Raspberry Cream Ale (wheat-based) is aromatic and, for a fruit beer, unusually strong (8%). The intensely fruity India Pale Ale offers a bold reminder of what you might have found aboard a British ship bound for India in the 19th century. Bigger still is the incredibly complex and flavorful Russian Imperial Stout (dry hopped). The hugely malty No. 1 Barley Wine, brewed with fireweed honey, shows rich caramelized notes from an incredible six-hour boil.

As this book went to press, Tall Ship's debt load had left the brewery's future in doubt. It is to be hoped that its distinctive brews will survive in one form or another.

Big ales in not-so-small bottles: Tall Ship's beers all check in at greater than 7% alcohol by volume. Tall, indeed!

EST. 1996
806 Coronation
Avenue,
Kelowna,
B.C. V1Y 7A3
Tel: (250) 860-8836

RECOMMENDED
Spy Dark Lager
(5%), dry, roasty,
and raisiny
Spiced
Midwinter Ale
(7%), ginger
snaps meet
mincemeat

TREE BREWING COMPANY

★

In the early days of British Columbia's micro movement, most brewery start-ups occurred on the lower mainland around Vancouver. The Okanagan Spring Brewery bucked this trend in 1985, however, instead establishing operations in the province's less populated interior. And recently, this mainly-agricultural region to the west of the Canadian Rockies has been proving as hospitable to new breweries as it historically has been for B.C.'s abundant orchards.

Standing tall among the new wave of inland micros is Tree Brewing, the brainchild of biologist Geoff Twyman. Twyman was lured to craft-brewing from a background in the province's burgeoning Okanagan winery business.

He remained in the interior, he says, in order to avoid the bureaucratic entanglements expected in cities such as Vancouver or Calgary. Nevertheless, shortly after Tree opened, Twyman got his taste of big city business when he listed the company on Vancouver's Stock Exchange.

Tree's original and flagship brand is the sweetish and peachy Amber Ale, which was followed to the market by a lightly-hopped, "round" Blonde Lager. The distinctive German dunkel-style Spy Dark Lager came next, offering an enjoyable spicy complexity. Tree's Red Ale, a moderately hoppy, plummy brew, rounded out the year-round range until the recent launch of an English-style pale ale. Tree's Spiced Midwinter Ale offers a burst of cold-weather character. It hopefully foreshadows Tree branching out into range of interesting seasonals. Production approached 6,000 barrels (7,000hl) in 1998.

Twisted Tree Pale Ale, brewed with five malts and East Kent Goldings, was launched in 1998.

EST. 1985
2330 Government St.,
Victoria,
B.C. V8T 5G5
Tel: (250) 361 0007

RECOMMENDED
Hermann's
Dark Lager
(5.5%), light, pleasant
chocolate and
caramel notes
Hermannator
(9%), eagerly-
awaited, supremely
hearty winter
seasonal

VANCOUVER ISLAND

A nother early Canadian micro. Founded on Vancouver Island in an industrial location lacking aesthetic appeal, the brewery originally operated as "Island Pacific." Its subsequent change of name and site – to new digs near downtown Victoria, capital city of B.C. – were instituted to help overcome what Canadian beer expert Stephen Beaumont called its status as "the forgotten player" in the country's craft-brewing history.

If Vancouver Island has suffered from a low profile, the fault does not lie with its beers. Respected German brewer Hermann Hoerterer developed many of the main brands. Although Herr Hermann has moved on, the beers (by their very names) still testify to his influence. A recent refocus of marketing efforts has boosted the brewery's sales and recognition in its home market, with a knock-on effect in Vancouver proper.

Vancouver Island Premium Lager, the company flagship, heads a small family that includes the sweetly fruity Piper's Pale Ale and the mainstreamish Blonde Ale. Hermann's Dark Lager, surely one of the better German-inspired dunkels brewed in Canada (along with Tree's Spy), offers smooth, chocolatey flavors before a balanced, bittersweet finish. The brewery sadly has discontinued its alliterative (well, for German speakers) Victoria Weizen — a good example of the filtered Bavarian style. Thankfully, Hermannator remains: this hugely characterful winter brew has alternated between doppelbock and eisbock status over the years. Regardless of its annual incarnation, it always is in short supply and high demand.

The most scenic route to Vancouver Island is via ferry through the San Juan Islands from the B.C. mainland.

Also worth trying

British Columbia capital Victoria hosts two of western Canada's best brewpubs. **Spinnakers**, the first modern "in house" brewpub in Canada, opened in 1984. A wide rotating selection features several truly cask-conditioned ales. Standards like Doc Hadfield's Pale Ale (with an excellent "fresh hop" character) support more exotic offerings such as a well-made Tsarist Imperial Stout and deliberately-soured "lambic." Victoria's other famous brewpub is **Buckerfield's Brewery**, informally known as Swan's because it is part of the attractive, lively Swan Hotel complex. Both its darkly-malty Scotch Ale and exceptionally smooth Oatmeal Stout, pleasantly roasty and bitter, are far more interesting than the quaffable Buckerfield's Bitter.

For a broad selection of regional micros, head to downtown Victoria's Sticky Wicket pub (919 Douglas Street, in the Strathcona Hotel).

Savvy Vancouver drinkers rejoice over the fruity-hoppy, sweetish Red Sky Alt Bier and hoppy, edge-of-control Hurricane IPA from the city's **Storm Brewing**, a tiny operation that opened in 1995. The city's two mainstay brewpubs, **Yaletown** and **Steam Works**, have produced somewhat variable-quality beers in the past, although the former has been more consistently impressive of late. On Granville Island, the **Creek Brewing** brewpub founded in 1997) is off to a promising start. Outposts of the Fogg n' Suds pub chain, based in the city, serve a decent selection of Canadian micros on tap.

North of Vancouver, open fermenters at **Horseshoe Bay Brewing** produce draft-only brews such as the flagship Bay Ale, Pale Ale, and potent (7%) Triple Frambozen. Still farther north, **Whistler Brewing** refreshes skiers and snowboarders with its Black Tusk Ale (really more of a dark lager) and soft, "artistic" Whistler Mother's Pale Ale. In the province's interior, **Mount Begbie Brewing** produces a laudable, draft only Kölsch, **Bear Brewing** offers a satisfying Black Bear Ale, and **Nelson Brewing** crafts a dry Black-heart Stout and hoppy Paddywhack India Pale Ale.

Across the provincial border, Alberta's **Banff Brewery** bucks the English-ale trend with German-style brews, including Banff Hefeweizen and Storm Mountain Bavarian Dark. Calgary's **Wild Rose Brewing** is making a mark on Big Rock's home turf with an impressive selection of draft ales, while the city's **Buzzards Cafe** offers its own Buzzard's Breath Ale (brewed by Big Rock) and a solid selection of micros on tap.

371

CANADA EAST

Eastern Canada's history swims in ale. After all, it was the beer style *du jour* of early settlers and the French Regime of the 17th century. During the next 200 years, the influence of English, Scottish, and Irish brewers only enhanced this ale tradition. Even as lager became Canada's national style, the eastern regions retained a taste for top-fermented brews that made the area fertile territory for imports and the most flavorful offerings of big domestic brewers.

Today, Québec hosts the most dynamic segment of Canada's craft-brewing industry, with Ontario running a slightly distant second. Micros abound, although the Atlantic provinces of Newfoundland, Prince Edward Island, Nova Scotia and New Brunswick only recently have joined the beer renaissance. And with a few exceptions – Brasal's rich Bock and Creemore Springs eponymous Lager, for example – ales remain the favored style.

Tastes embrace everything from the hoppy (McAuslan's St. Ambroise Pale) to the malty (Hart's Festive Brown) to the cutting-edge creat-ive (Unibroue's Belgian-inspired ales and Cheval Blanc's quirky brews). Jean Talon, an early Québec governor who built a brewery in order to reduce the province's dependence on imported drink, would be proud.

EST. 1989
8477, Rue Cordner,
Lasalle,
Montréal,
Québec M8N 2X2
Tel: (514) 365 5050

RECOMMENDED
Special Amber
(6.1%), "über
Vienna," or
nut-brown lager?
Brasal Bock
(7.8%), seamlessly
smooth,
outstandingly
flavorful

BRASAL BREWING
(Brasserie Brasal)

A "culturally challenging" micro: located in French Canada, founded by two Austrians, producing Bavarian-inspired lagers. The name is a contraction of Brasserie Allemagne ("German Brewery"). Despite Québec's taste for ale, or perhaps because of it, the owners saw a niche market for fresh, locally-

RIGHT: *Bottle after bottle after bottle of Brasal beer – bock, perhaps – on their way to grateful consumers.*

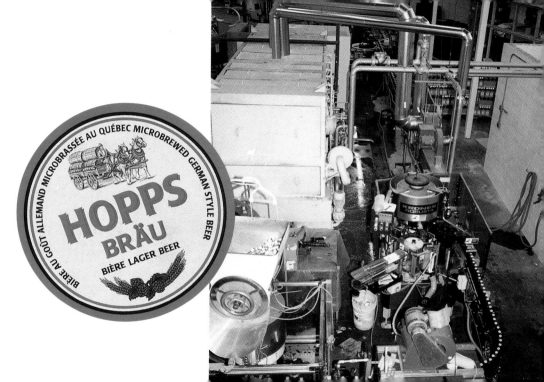

brewed lager beers like those of their homeland. Today, Brasal claims a substantial craft-beer market share in the province.

Exports to neighboring Ontario, Alberta, and, more signifcantly, America also are growing. An agreement with World Class Beer Imports has established Brasal's beers in key United States markets from Washington DC to

Seattle. The brewery's 1997 production was close to 14,000 barrels (16,400hl).

Brasal takes pains to note that all of its beers are made according to the *Reinheitsgebot* (the Bavarian purity law). Drinkers will be more impressed by the character of Brasal's brews, which is uniformly good. The flagship Hopps Bräu, a fresh-tasting (and slightly "muscular") Pilsner, clearly illustrates the brewery's founding purpose. Brasal's big-bodied Special Amber boasts a Vienna lager's spiciness, the nutty flavors of a brown ale, and a potency greater than either. Best is the rich ruby-colored Bock – lagered for three months – with its coffee, caramel, and lightly fruity

notes. A top example of the dunkel-bock style, it should help Québec ale-o-philes learn to love lagers. Other Brasal brands include Hopps aux Pommes (an apple-flavored lager at 4.1%), as well as Hek Rousse (an amber lager brewed for a regional super-market chain) and a low-alcohol/low-calorie Light.

Brasal is multi-national brewing: Austrian founders, German-style beers, labels in English and French.

BRICK BREWING COMPANY

EST. 1984
181 King Street
South,
Waterloo,
Ontario N2J 1P7
Tel: (519) 576-9100

RECOMMENDED
Andechs Spezial
Hell Lager
(5%), wonderfully
balanced,
fragrant hop,
delicate malt
Anniversary Bock
(7.8%),
decadently rich
and warming

Eastern Canada's first modern microbrewery, Brick opened (on founder Jim Brickman's birthday) with a mission to brew German-inspired lagers for the largely Germanic population of the town once known as Berlin, Ontario. Brickman himself was oft-quoted as saying that he would never allow his brewery to produce ales because he wasn't personally fond of them.

How times, people and breweries

Andechs is a famous brewing monastery outside of Munich. Brick's version saves Canadians the pilgrimage.

379

ABOVE: *Brick bought Algonquin in 1997, but has kept the facility operating instead of moving production to its own plant.*

change! Today, Brick Brewing counts itself among the largest regional breweries in Canada and produces over two dozen different beers, about a quarter of them ales. Many of these brands came to the company during Brick's acquisition frenzy of 1996–1997, when the company purchased the struggling Conners

and Algonquin craft breweries, assumed the rights to the mainstream Laker family of beers, and reached agreements to brew Celis White (from Celis Brewing of Texas) and Andechs Spezial Hell (from Klosterbrauerie Andechs of Germany) for Canada. Close to the same time, national giant Molson Brewing purchased around a 19 percent stake in the brewery.

Of Brick's many brands, some of the best populate its portfolio of licensed beers: the perfumey, floral Andechs, the orangey Celis, and the lightly grassy, moderately hoppy Henninger Kaiser Pilsner Lager. Standouts among the brewery's mainstay brands include Brick's seasonal Anniversary Bock, with its brandy-ish alcohol and dark chocolate richness, and the refreshing Brick Premium Lager. The Conners brands feature a lightly citric Best Bitter and Conners Ale (a brown ale full of black cherry, chocolate notes).

Wine drinkers should not confuse Brick's with "Brix," a measure of (residual) sugar in grape juice or wine.

EST. 1937,1995
5020 St. Patrick,
Montréal,
Québec H4E 1A5
Tel: (514) 362-1551

RECOMMENDED
Coup de Grisou
(5%), spicy,
exploding with
flavor
Ambrée
Traditionale
(5%), nutty,
toasty, eminently
drinkable

CHEVAL BLANC BREWERY
(Brasserie le Cheval Blanc)

The very first modern brewpub to open in Montréal was the Cheval Blanc, located in the heart of downtown at 809 Ontario Street East. Or perhaps "opened" is not the right word; the old taverne had been in Jerôme Denys' family since its founding in 1937. His interest in craft-brewed beer prompted the Cheval's rebirth as a brewpub.

One of the more interesting aspects of the early Cheval Blanc beer was that Denys modified each of his recipes every three months or so, in effect making each of the house beers into a "seasonal." This somewhat eccentric approach to brewing earned Denys a positive reputation for his unusual and seasonal beers when the Cheval Blanc began to bottle in 1992. It still serves him well at his new brewery in the city's south end.

All of the Cheval Blanc beers are bottle-conditioned and most are at least a bit unusual. The flagship

brands are the most conventional: a spicy, well-coriandered Blanche Originale ("Original White"), a spicy-fruity Rousse Legendaire ("Legendary Red"), and a nutty Ambrée Traditionale ("Traditional Amber"). Among the more unusual offerings are a buckwheat beer called Coup de Grisou, a strong maple ale named Tord-Vis (named after a maple-sap tapping device), and a cranberry-and-spice winter ale titled Snoreau.

Denys also has been licensed to use yeast from Brasserie d'Achouffe, a farmhouse micro in Belgium, with which he crafts a lightly spicy, orangey Blonde d'Achouffe.

ABOVE: *Inside the bar of the Cheval Blanc, which usually is crammed with patrons drinking the house-brewed ales.*

Excepting Coup de Grisou, Cheval Blanc has yet to brew a beer with any "Little Rascal" ingredients.

EST. 1987
139 Mill Street,
Creemore,
Ontario L0M 1G0
Tel: (705) 466 2240

RECOMMENDED
Premium Lager
(5%), exceptionally
well-rounded and
fresh-tasting

CREEMORE SPRINGS BREWERY

Creemore, a rural town around two hours north of Toronto, isn't quite as bucolic as it first appears: many of the sleepy houses belong to big-city escapees or vacationers. Operating out of the town's converted 1890's "May Hardware Store," Creemore Springs Brewery is a thriving example of doing only one thing extremely well. Unlike almost every other craft-brewer in North America, Creemore specializes in only one beer: the unusually malty, floral Creemore Springs Premium Lager.

Reportedly inspired by Pilsner Urquell, Creemore Springs Lager is deeper and fuller bodied – less a Pilsner than an extremely fresh-tasting amber lager. Its soft, full flavor (a balance between sweetish, faintly nutty malt, and floral, spicy hops) is

5% alc / vol — 500 ml

BREWED WITH ALL THE GOOD STUFF AND LOTS OF TENDER LOVING CARE

CREEMORE SPRINGS

Since 1987

PREMIUM LAGER

CLEAR SPRING WATER • PREMIUM MALT • SPECIALTY HOPS • SELECT YEAST
NO ADDITIVES • NO PRESERVATIVES • NO PASTEURIZATION

best appreciated on draft. To this end, Creemore Springs sold only kegs for more than a year after opening. The result was a powerful demand for its beer on tap at restaurants in bars throughout its home region and into greater Toronto. Premium Lager is now sold in bottle-conditioned form in some export markets.

In 1996, Creemore broke with its single beer tradition and introduced the brewery's first, and to date only, seasonal: Creemore Springs ur-Bock, a wintertime "warmer." Perhaps a shade too conservatively crafted in its first year, this full-bodied dark bock developed into a roasty, flavorful contender in 1997.

> Creemore Springs makes the kind of fresh, satisfying lager that most of North America's big brewers pretend they do.

175 Industrial Avenue,
Carleton Place,
Ontario
Tel: (613) 253 4278

RECOMMENDED
Dragon's Breath
Pale Ale
(4.5%), fresh hop
aroma and character
Hart Amber Ale
(5%), complex fruit
and toasty malt
Hart Festive
Brown Ale
(6%), nutty, spicy,
lots of smooth
depth

HART BREWING

★

This is the premier Ottawa Valley micro, whose presence is particularly strong throughout eastern Ontario and into Toronto. Founder Lorne Hart, a retired engineer, established the brewery after a market analysis showed that the Ottawa area could support such a project. Despite a few lean early years – the Ottawa region was not as thirsty as Hart's analysis had anticipated! – the com-pany's bottom line has been buoyed recently by its sale of a majority interest to Montréal-based Upland Global Corporation. Production approached 8,500 barrels (10,000hl) in 1998.

Hart's flagship Amber Ale and several other beers were formulated by peripatetic brewmaster Alan Pugsley (in his pre-Shipyard days). The Amber offers a smooth toasty-malt character with plenty

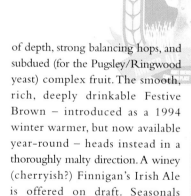

of depth, strong balancing hops, and subdued (for the Pugsley/Ringwood yeast) complex fruit. The smooth, rich, deeply drinkable Festive Brown – introduced as a 1994 winter warmer, but now available year-round – heads instead in a thoroughly malty direction. A winey (cherryish?) Finnigan's Irish Ale is offered on draft. Seasonals include fall's Pumpkin Ale, a winter Stout, and springtime Maple Brown ale. Hart also produces kegs and bottles of Dragon's Breath Pale (hoppy, IPA-like) under license for the Kingston Brewing Company brewpub, as well as bottles of Peculiar (a roasty old ale) for Toronto's Granite brewpub.

Upon buying into the brewery, Upland Global's first move was to refocus the marketing of Hart in the Ottawa Valley. The new owners are hoping local consumers, more than anyone else, will want to "have a Hart."

Bi-national beer confusion was cured in 1996, when Seattle's Hart Brewing officially changed its name to Pyramid.

EST. 1989
4850 Rue St.
Ambroise, Montréal,
Québec H4C 3N8
Tel: (514) 939 6139

RECOMMENDED
Griffon Extra
Pale Ale
(5%), softly fruity,
clean honeyed malt
St. Ambroise
Pale Ale
(5%), pleasantly
(somewhat
aggressively) hoppy
St. Ambroise
Oatmeal Stout
(5.5%), excellent dry
example of style

MᶜAUSLAN BREWING
(Brasserie McAuslan)

McAuslan is one of the best known names in Canadian craft brewing. Founder Peter McAuslan homebrewed for years before making the leap from college administrator to professional microbrewer. Itinerant brewer Alan Pugsley helped McAuslan build his plant and develop the recipe for St. Ambroise Pale, the

original brew. Today, brewing is supervised by Ellen Bounsall, a trained biologist who happens to be McAuslan's wife. McAuslan's beers now are available widely in Québec and Ontario, as well as the United States. The brewery is expected to produce more than 17,000 barrels (20,000hl) in 1998.

All of McAuslan's

RIGHT: *French-speaking drinkers enjoy this soft, fruity, quaffable Blonde, and nor are the English-speakers complaining!*

389

5% alc./vol.
341 mL

www.mcauslan.com

MCAUSLAN

LA BRASSERIE MCAUSLAN BREWING INC. RUE SAINT-AMBROISE, MONTRÉAL, QUÉBEC

Bière de blé à l'abricot
Apricot Wheat Ale

beers have a more restrained character than others brewed with the Ringwood yeast and Peter Austin equipment (the Pugsley connection). The St. Ambroise beers are the most distinctive: the Pale bursts with citric hop character over lightly toasty malt and complex fruit; the flagship Oatmeal Stout, drier and more coffeeish than many examples, balances its smooth character with strong roasted notes. McAuslan's Griffon line, purposely designed to be "more accessible," includes the soft, quaffable Extra Pale and a caramel-accented, medium-bodied Brown Ale. In addition, McAuslan makes an "extra special pale ale" (ESP?) called Frontenac for the local Québec market.

In 1998, the company began to introduce several new specialties: a potent Scotch Ale (7.2%, sold through government liquor stores), for example, as well as a draft-only Cream Ale dispensed with nitrogen. Four seasonals, such as winter's Bière Forte (Strong Ale) and spring's Apricot Wheat, also are offered.

RIGHT: *The trademark brick-clad brewkettle reveals the role that Peter Austin played in McAuslan's design.*

McAuslan was an early Canadian brewer to find sales success south of the border in America.

EST. 1989
6863 Lundy's Lane,
Niagara Falls,
Ontario L2G 1V7
Tel: (905) 374 1166

RECOMMENDED
Brock's Extra Stout
(5.8%), deliciously
coffeeish,
incredibly roasty,
Scotch Ale
(7.2%), big and
malty; lingering,
warming finish
Eisbock
(8%), an annual
brew well worth
seeking

This colorful micro is not so far east of the famous Falls (so far, no one has gone over in one of the brewery's barrels!). It was founded by two brothers who previously operated a brewery in Addis Ababa, Ethiopia, along with a few partners with a background in the region's wine industry. While a mainstream-oriented Trapper Premium Lager (since discontinued) was the brewery's first brand, their claim to fame arrived with the launch of their second, the winter seasonal Niagara Falls Eisbock. This potent, concentrated, vintage-dated brew remains the brewery's trademark brand, but

accounted for only a modest portion of their 7,500 barrels (9,000hl) of 1997 production. It has tended to be more quaffable than classic German examples of the style.

The best-seller for Niagara Falls is their spicy-nutty and fruity (orange/apricot) Gritstone Premium Ale, which represented over half of the brew-

ery's 1997 production. The specialty Brock's Extra Stout tastes powerfully of roasted grain, with hints of licorice, while a strong ale called Old Jack is smooth, sweetish and blessed with Gritstone-type fruitiness. Niagara Falls Premium Lager and Light are the most mainstream of the brewery's brands. The summer seasonal, draft Weisse, is likewise approachable with its lightly citric notes. Far bigger and more interesting is Niagara's Scotch Ale, a creamy, lightly-peaty winter warmer available on draft.

In the summer of 1998, Canada's Premium Beer Company (owned by long-time brewer Moosehead) assumed jurisdiction over the sales and marketing of Niagara Falls' beers and was reportedly considering the possible purchase of the brewery.

Eisbock

The ice bridge of Niagara Falls was our inspiration for this unique award-winning ice beer. This bock-style beer is made by freezing the beer and removing the ice, producing a remarkable delicate, full-bodied beer for you to enjoy this winter 95-96.

Strong Beer   Bière Forte

8% alc./vol.   750mL

EST. 1995
135-D, Chemin
du Tremblay,
Boucherville,
Québec J4B 7K4
Tel: (514) 641 6433

RECOMMENDED
Seigneuriale
(7.5%), dry-hopped,
fruity, deliciously
complex ale
**Seigneuriale
Reserve**
(7.5%), similar
to Seigneuriale,
spicier and
earthier

SEIGNEURIALE BREWERY
(Brasserie Seigneuriale)

Part of the second generation of Québec craft breweries that cropped up in the mid-1990's, Seigneuriale was more than three years in the making. For starters, the father-and-son team of Marcel and Guy Laflamme spent several months in Belgium during 1992 while Guy trained at a half-dozen different breweries. Upon their return, the

duo began developing a test-brewery and experimenting with recipes. By 1994, they were ready to incorporate their brewery, and in June of 1995, the first bottles of the flagship Seigneuriale appeared in public. The brewery's name refers to a kind of royal land-grant given to early Canadian colonists.

Seigneuriale's arrival was one of the most critically lauded debuts for any Canadian craft brewery this decade. Best described as a uniquely Québécois take on a strong Belgian ale, the beer was acclaimed in the pages of numerous publications (including the respected enophile journal *Wine Enthusiast*). The rest of Seigeuriale's quartet of strong, bottle-conditioned ales include Seigneuriale Reserve (the original beer's drier, earthier brother), a honey-influenced and strong-yet-oddly-refreshing Seigneuriale Blonde, and a big and fruity Seigneuriale Triple. All are packaged in half-liter bottles.

In the summer of 1998, Ontario-based Sleeman Breweries purchased the Seigneuriale Brewery and issued a promise that the existing beer recipes would not be compromised. Ale-lovers are watching closely to see the results. Benefits could be expanded distribution and production; the small company brewed only 3,400 barrels (4,000hl) in 1997.

Historically, the Seigneuriale extended to the Lord's pick of the maidens on his property. But what about the beer?

397

EST. 1990
80, Des Carrières
Chambly,
Québec J3L 2H6
Tel: (514) 658 7658

RECOMMENDED
Blanche de Chambly
(5%), fragrant, lemony, pleasantly tart Belgian "white"
Maudite
(8%), peppery, faintly minty, richly malty
Quelque Chose
(8%), wonderfully-balanced spiced cherry ale

UNIBROUE BREWING

★

An aesthetically-minded micro making Belgian-inspired ales, founded after the owner reached an arrangement with Belgium's Riva brewery to produce their Dentergems Witbier recipe in Canada (the beer which became Blanche de Chambly). The company aggressively has expanded both production and distribution, creating its own subsidiary importers in both America and France.

All of Unibroue's ales are bottle-conditioned, often with several months bottle-aging behind them. The flagship Blanche de Chambly ("White of Chambly") is deliciously dry, "wheaty," and citrus-tart with vanilla notes – neither as soft as Hoegaarden, nor as firm as Celis. Maudite ("Damned") takes its

RAFTMAN

BEER ON LEES FROM WHISKY MALT

5.5% alc./vol.
1 PT. 9.4 FL. OZ.

UNIBROUE INC. CHAMBLY QUEBEC

BLANCHE DE

CHAMBLY

WHITE BEER ON LEES
12 FL. OZ. (355 ML)
5% alc./vol.

BOTTLE REFERMENTATION

Unibroue's
stronger beers,
particularly
Maudite and La
Fin du Monde, age
well if stored
properly.

399

Maudite's label shows trappers in a flying canoe – its supernatural transportation is part of their devilish deal.

name from a French Canadian legend about trappers who sold their souls in order to make it home for a party: it is smooth and malty-rich with spicy accents. La Fin du Monde ("The End of the World"), which falls between a strong golden ale (think Duvel) and a Belgian tripel, offers a more finessed, honeyish malt character. Eau Benite ("Holy Water") is cast more in the typical Belgian tripel-style mold, with a drier, firmer character.

Unibroue also brews a faintly smoky "whisky malt" beer called Raftman, a delicate, cleanly malty, spicy La Gaillarde (a spiced ale in the "medieval style"), the big, chocolatey Trois Pistoles, and an incredibly full-flavored, spiced cherry beer called Quelque Chose ("Something"), designed to be served hot. For the first time, Unibroue has expanded outside of its range of distinctive ales with a Pilsner-style brew simply called "U."

EST. 1985
950 Woodlawn Rd. W.
Guelph,
Ontario N1K 1B8
Tel: (519) 837 2337

RECOMMENDED
Arkell Best Bitter
(4%), at its best when
cask-conditioned
County Ale
(5%), fruity but
well-balanced amber
Iron Duke
(6.5%), strong, malty,
nutty complexity

WELLINGTON COUNTY BREWERIES

This early Ontario micro was established by a group of British ale enthusiasts to provide locally-brewed, authentic cask–conditioned ales – a noble plan that hit a major snag after the first casks of Best Bitter and County Ale rolled out the door. The majority of area publicans, it seemed, were either unable or unwilling to provide the extra effort needed to serve true "real ale."

Arthur Wellesley, the 1st Duke of Wellington, lived from 1769 to 1852. He was a British general and statesman.

Wellington quickly (and successfully) began offering filtered ales in standard kegs and bottles. Nevertheless, perhaps in part due to its early difficulties, the brewery remains relatively small. Production was expected to reach 8,500 barrels (10,000hl) in 1998, with distribution throughout southern Ontario.

A handful of accounts still serve Wellington's original Arkell Best Bitter (a dry, hoppy session brew) and County Ale in cask-conditioned form. A Special Cream Pale Ale, between the two in strength, offers a "more approachable" character. The brewery's flagship Iron Duke Strong Ale, a robust reddish ale with layers of

malt flavor, recently has been joined by a pair of siblings: a dryish, roasty Iron Duke Strong Porter and a rich, intense Iron Duke Imperial Stout. The company also offers a well made Premium Lager in the Vienna style, and a popular Honey Lager. All of Wellington's ales are unified by English-favored ingredients like East Kent (and Styrian) Golding hops. Which means that, despite their rare cask appearances, they still offer the originally-envisioned taste of Britain.

Also worth trying

Québec drinkers say *oui* to a host of French-accented brews, including the Vienna-style Belle Gueule lager and Canon doppelbock from **Brasserie GMT**; the softly floral Boréale Blonde, malty Boréale Rousse and well-roasted Boréale Noire from **Les Brasseurs du Nord**; the quirky, maple-flavored La Beauceronne à l'Érable from **Ferme Brasserie Schoune**; and the offerings from several good brewpubs, including a particularly clean and crisp Pilsner from Montréal's **l'Amere à Boire.**

Ontario also offers several additional suds of note, including the excellent Brown Ale, satisfying Pale Ale and refreshing Raspberry Wheat from **Kawartha Lakes Brewing**. British traditionalists in Toronto may prefer the dry-hopped Best Bitter from Toronto's **Granite Brewery** brewpub, while weizen enthusiasts will welcome the German-style Wheat Beer at **Denison's Brewing** brewpub. Aficionados of more unusual styles will enjoy the Elora Rye from the **Old Mill Brewery**, located in Elora.

The Atlantic provinces, long a dormant craft beer market, have recently come alive with the opening of several breweries and brew-pubs, including **Freshwater Brewing** and **Quidi Vidi Brewing** in Newfoundland, **Picaroons Brewing** of New Brunswick, **Maritime Beer** and **Propeller Brewing** of Nova Scotia, and the **Lone Star Cafe and Brewery** on tiny Prince Edward Island. Always worth a stop if you are in Halifax, Nova Scotia, is the venerable **Granite Brewery** brewpub, older brother to the Toronto version.

Until recently, Canadian law restricted domestic brewers to selling beer in provinces where they operated a brewery

Alcohol

A by-product of fermentation. Beer's alcohol content today is commonly expressed as "by volume" – a percentage measure of the amount of pure alcohol in a given volume of beer. All measurements of alcohol (e.g., 5.5%) in this book are by volume unless otherwise noted.

Ale

Any beer fermented with yeast that "works" at relatively warm temperatures (approximately 60-75°F; 15-24°C). Warm temperatures encourage both yeast activity – creating relatively rapid fermentations – and the production of aromatic and/or flavor compounds (esters). Some popular ale styles include pale ale, wheat beer, porter, stout, and barley wine.

Barrel

While any large beer container can be called a barrel, brewers use the term to define a standardized volume of production. In America, a "barrel" holds 31 US gallons (117.3 liters) of beer. The standard American "keg" is a half-barrel (15.5 gallons, 58.7 liters); a "pony" keg is a quarter-barrel (7.75 gallons, 29.3 liters).

Beer

Any fermented beverage made from grain. Almost all modern beers are seasoned with hops. But for much of civilization's brewing history, other flavorings – honey, dates, nutmeg, pepper, and far stranger substances – were employed. Beer divides into two basic categories, ales and lagers, just like wine is split into red and white.

Brewpub

A pub or restaurant with an on-site brewery, serving the majority of its beer to customers on the premises.

BUs

(Bitterness Units) A scale for recording the bitterness of beer. Because the BU figure is based on an analysis of the parts per million of "isomerized" alpha acids in a beer (see "Hops"), it does not directly correlate to perceived bitterness – the level of bitterness discerned by a drinker.

Cask

A manually-tapped barrel or keg. Beer that experiences a final fermentation, resulting in natural carbonation, in such a container is called "cask-conditioned" (the same process in a bottle is "bottle-conditioning"). Hand-pumps traditionally are used to serve cask beer.

Craft-Brewery

See "Microbrewery."

Dry Hopping

The process of steeping hops (blossoms or pellets) in a maturing or finished beer, in order to impart extra aroma and flavor to the brew.

Fermentation

The process in which yeast cells feed on sugar, giving off alcohol and carbon dioxide (fizz!) as by-products. "Top fermentation" and "bottom fermentation" are outdated terms used to indicate, respectively, warm (ale) or cool (lager) fermentation.

Hops

Flowers, frequently called "blossoms" or "cones," of a climbing vine (*Humulus lupulus*) used to give beer its bitter flavors and herbal aromas. Hops contain lupulin, a complex substance that includes aromatic oils and "alpha acids" (compounds that impart bitterness to beer). Just like grapes, different hop varieties have different aroma and flavor characteristics.

Lager

Any beer fermented with yeast that "works" at relatively low temperatures (approximately 40-50°F, 4-10°C). These cool temperatures discourage both yeast activity – creating fairly lengthy fermentations – and the production of ale-like aromatic and/or flavor compounds. Some popular lager styles include Pilsner, bock, Vienna/amber, and doppelbock.

Malt

Cereal grain that has been partially germinated and then heat-dried to a level of "toasty" consistency. Barley malt generally is used for beer-making, along with "specialty" malts like wheat and rye. Industrial brewers typically supplement malt with unmalted "adjunct" grains such as rice and corn.

Mash

The mixture of grain (called the "grist") and hot water at the start of the brewing process.

Microbrewery

A small brewery. America's Association of Brewers currently defines "microbrewery" as a facility producing fewer than 15,000 US barrels per year. The term "craft-brewery" refers to companies above this production level that continue to produce beers consistent with the "micro" philosophy (making beers across a broad range of historic and/or innovative styles).

Original Gravity (OG)

The specific gravity of a beer before fermentation, measuring its density compared to that of pure water. The higher a beer's original gravity, the greater its amount of fermentable material (sugar).

Reinheitsgebot

German "purity law" (codified in 1516) restricting beer ingredients to malt, hops, yeast, and water.

Wort

Pronounced "wert." The sugar-rich liquid derived from the mash, then boiled with hops in the brewkettle.

Yeast

A single-celled organism responsible for fermentation. Most modern brewers use specially-cultivated "ale" or "lager" yeasts, depending on the style of beer they wish to make.

412

414